My First, Second & Third Attempts at Parenting

Discovering the Heart of Parenting

PRAISE FOR
My First, Second & Third Attempts at Parenting

Steve Murrell is a man to be taken seriously no matter what he's talking about, but especially when he speaks about the heart of fathering.

— **Dr. Chuck Quinley**
Missionary
Author of *Simple Parenting*

This book is a gift to anyone who needs someone to come alongside them on the parenting journey. You will be inspired and encouraged.

— **Eddie Lyons**
Senior Pastor, High Street Baptist Church
President, Baptist Bible Fellowship International

This is not a book about being perfect or raising perfect children; rather, it inspires, reminds, and guides us to focus on the inside — to raise up a younger generation with a heart after God.

— **Marie Bonifacio**
Next-door Neighbor

It has been a blessing and inspiration to witness the way Steve and Deborah Murrell raised their three sons — William, James, and Jonathan! The boys were always top priority for them. This book is a precious gift to parents yearning to be guided in bringing up their children in the Lord's ways!

— **Coney Reyes**
Family Friend and Actress

I can't say enough good things about being the third attempt. The curve was well-established, my parents' defenses were worn down and standards lax, cookies were left unguarded, bedtimes were more theory than actual hard practice. But maybe all this had more to do with me being the favorite and not the third . . .

— **Jonathan Murrell**
The Third Attempt

A lot of people complain or feel bad about being a middle child, but it was the best of both worlds for me. I could do things that my older brother could do, but I could also avoid responsibility when circumstances called for it. Life in the middle was pretty perfect.

— **James Murrell**
The Second Attempt

This book explains a lot.

— **William Murrell**
The First Attempt

I hope that all who get to read this book will benefit from these tales as much as I did. I realize that while Pastor Steve's brand of parenting may sound simple, it definitely isn't easy; and like all things, only truly accomplishable by the grace of God.

— **Carla Peralejo-Bonifacio**
Family Friend, Actress, and Blogger

William married my precious daughter, and I saw in him a humble and caring Christ-centered spirit. His father, Steve, is a humble man who has been blessed with a beautiful family and God-inspired wisdom regarding what's really important in raising our children in the way they should go. I have been truly humbled by reading this book!

— **Dr. Robert Baily**
Father-in-Law to William Murrell

Ako ay nagagalak at may isang aklat na makakatulong sumubay-bay sa mga nakababatang magulang. Basahin, samantalahin, at tuparin ang payo ng isang bihasang ama. Ang aking apo ay pinagpala na makasama sa pamilyang ito.

— **Alejandro Nogoy**
Grandfather-in-Law to Jonathan Murrell

My First, Second & Third Attempts at Parenting

Discovering the Heart of Parenting

Steve Murrell

DEDICATION

To William, James, and Jonathan —
my first, second, and third attempts at parenting.
Thank you for filling our lives with love, joy,
and endless adventure. Thank you for filling
our home with music, our walls with art, and
our dinner table with laughter. Thank you for always
honoring your mother and me with your words and actions.
And most of all, thank you for living to please God.

My First, Second & Third Attempts at Parenting
Copyright © 2015 by Steve Murrell
All rights reserved

For information on sales, licensing, or permissions,
contact the publisher:
Mill City Press
322 First Avenue N, Suite 500
Minneapolis, MN 55401

1-888-MILL CITY

Trade Paperback ISBN: 978-1-63413-861-1

CONTENTS

INTRODUCTION

THE PURPOSE-DRIVEN BOOK
What This Book is Not

Throughout my parenting career, I've read a lot of parenting books. Some helped me. Some did not. Most were practical how-to books detailing best practices for family devotions, behavioral discipline, preparing toddlers for the Ivy League, and other parenting essentials.

This book, however, is about the elusive part of parenting—the heart. Chapter by chapter, story by story, we will examine God's heart toward children, our hearts as parents, and how to shape a child's heart. Plenty of parenting books focus on how to fix bad behavior. Not so many focus on how to cultivate a child's heart. Even fewer focus on how to deal with our own hearts as parents. Training children to obey is important, but it's more important that they have a heart to follow God.

My goal in writing this book is that people will understand God's heart for children and will catch the heart of parenting.

My First, Second & Third Attempts at Parenting is the opposite of a how-to book. It's intentionally more philosophical than practical and more personal than academic. It's a collection of stories and experiences, rather than an exegetical Bible study.

Because I'm convinced that small group discipleship (a.k.a. community) is the best way to do life and family, each chapter ends with small group discussion questions.

Before deciding on *My First, Second & Third Attempts at Parenting* as the title, I considered several other options, including the following:

WikiChild — The obvious follow-up to *WikiChurch*, my book on discipleship.

100,000 Dollars from Now — The sequel to my last book, *100 Years from Now*, which would emphasize the cost of emergency room visits, piano lessons, and tennis coaches for my three sons.

Purple Parents — A title that makes almost as much sense as *The Purple Book*, the foundational Bible study book I coauthored with Dr. Rice Broocks.

Discipleship at Home — Because there can never be too many books on discipleship.

The Heart of Parenting — My choice, but I was told this was too generic and sounded more like a subtitle.

Dad's Not Dead (Yet) — Why not ride the wave created by the *God's Not Dead* book and movie?

Change the Diaper, Change the World — The campus ministry classic by Dr. Rice Broocks, *Change the Campus, Change the World*, had such an impact, why not position this book as the prequel? (Many years ago, I made a vow to God that after Jonathan was fully potty-trained, I would never again change a dirty diaper. Eighteen months into my career as a grandfather, I am proud to report that I have kept that vow.

So, while I still want to change the world, I'm leaving the "change the diaper" part to the next generation.)

After extensive market research (I asked Deborah what she thought), *My First, Second & Third Attempts at Parenting* became the title. Those three attempts are my sons: William, James, and Jonathan.

As you can see, the chapters are named after some of my favorite books. I've added a subtitle to each chapter to make sure everyone gets the point of the chapter (and to keep me from wandering too far off-topic).

This book originally had six chapters, based on a six-lesson *Heart of Parenting* seminar and small group discipleship guide that Deborah and I developed many years ago. But as soon as I started writing, the book started growing. The same thing often happens to my sermons.

The chapters are divided into three sections. The *History* section provides the context. The *Heart* section is the core teaching from our *Heart of Parenting* seminar. The *Home* section is the only part of this book that is even remotely practical. It's obviously about applying parenting principles at home.

Thank you for reading this book. I pray it helps you catch the heart of parenting so that you and your kids survive your first, second, and third attempts at parenting (with minimal permanent damage).

FOREWORD

THE THREE MUSKETEERS
What My Parents Did Right

A few years ago, I spoke at a parenting seminar with my parents. Having been in the ministry for decades, they had spoken at dozens of parenting seminars. Being twenty-five and single, this was my first one.

As I anxiously thought about what I was going to say to the 800 people who had signed up for the well-marketed church event, I fought the urge to merely recycle some of my dad's classic sermon illustrations featuring me. As is the case with most pastors' kids, many of my most glorious and inglorious childhood moments had been immortalized from the pulpit and later, the blogosphere. After searching my mental hard drive for new, untold childhood stories that would inspire—or at least entertain—the audience, I settled on three and attempted to link them with biblical principles about parenting. I rehearsed the stories, clarified my take-aways, and cobbled together a PowerPoint presentation.

But the more I thought about my rare public-speaking opportunity, the more I realized that no one really cared what I thought about parenting. I was there to give honest, unrehearsed commentary on how I thought my parents had done as parents.

Then it hit me — tens of thousands of people all over the world could comment on my parents as pastors. And dozens, maybe hundreds, of people could comment on my parents as mentors and friends. But only three people in the whole world (me and my two younger brothers) could comment on my parents as parents. And that is why I — an unmarried twenty-something with a degree in medieval history — was speaking at a parenting seminar.

And that's also why I'm writing this foreword.

However, today, three years later, I write as a new father — with a whopping five weeks of experience. Though my brief (yet life-altering) parenting experience doesn't qualify me to offer much beyond diaper-changing advice, it has made me think more seriously about how I was raised and how my wife and I want to raise our new daughter.

When I think about my dad and my mom and what they did right as parents, it's impossible to translate their parenting strengths into tidy bullet points and PowerPoint slides. Perhaps the simplest way to put it is this: they understood the heart of parenting.

They understood that parenting was about internal transformation, not external performance.

They didn't really care if my brothers and I won our baseball games or tennis matches. They cared if we had good attitudes — especially when we lost.

They didn't really care if we became great pianists — we didn't. They, or at least my mom, cared if we practiced every day.

They didn't really care if we were honor students — we were, sometimes. They cared if we tried our best in school.

They didn't really care if we followed their footsteps into ministry — none of us have. They cared if we loved Jesus, His Church, and its mission.

They didn't really care if we were model pastors' kids — sometimes we weren't. They cared if we lived a life that honored God.

Looking back, I'm so thankful that my parents focused primarily on our hearts rather than our behavior. They understood that parenting is all about the things that you can't see. It's about shaping attitudes, not performance. It's about instilling self-control, not parental control. It's about helping your children cultivate a heart for Jesus, not a squeaky-clean image.

Like all parents, my wife and I have big plans for our five-week-old.

We hope she's good at sports, tennis in particular. We hope that one day she'll play the piano and be an honor student and be involved in church and be successful in whatever she does. But more than any of those things, we hope she will love Jesus with her whole heart, soul, mind, and strength. And we pray that, as parents, we raise our daughter in a way that encourages, rather than hinders, her relationship with her heavenly Father.

If this is your prayer for your children, then this is your book.

— William S. Murrell, Jr.
February 1, 2014

HISTORY

1

GONE WITH THE WIND
Seize the Moment Before
the Moment is Gone

The Old South, look for it only in books, for it is no more than a dream remembered, a Civilization gone with the wind.

Introduction, *Gone with the Wind*

Man is like a breath; his days are like a passing shadow.

Psalm 144:4

. . . What is your life? For you are a mist that appears for a little time and then vanishes.

James 4:14

What started as a single tear escaping one eye quickly turned into a flash flood.

"Mom, are you okay?" Our eight-year-old son was concerned and maybe a bit embarrassed that his mother was crying in public for no apparent reason.

I knew exactly why she was crying, but I couldn't explain it to our sons who were eight, six, and four at the time. I knew they'd understand one day, but not until they had children of their own.

We had been to Manila's Ninoy Aquino International Airport a thousand times before to catch the ridiculously early flight from Manila to San Francisco. We'd never had an emotional outburst. Until that day.

As we waited in line to check our luggage and get our boarding passes, Deborah noticed a family huddled together at the point of no return (also known as the immigration counter). The mom and dad seemed to be saying goodbye to their fuzzy-faced teenage son.

The mom was crying. The dad was trying not to. One last hug from mom, an awkward handshake and shoulder pat from dad, and the son threw his backpack over his shoulder and marched toward the immigration officer, passport in one hand, ticket in the other. Mom and dad embraced. Mom sobbed. Dad bit his quivering lip in a last-ditch attempt to stop the tears. They left the airport together. Their son left the Philippines alone.

> We wish we had a pause button so we could freeze a million different moments with our sons. Or maybe a rewind button so we could relive those million moments.

The longer Deborah watched this scene unfold, the more she lost control of her tear ducts. Five more minutes and she would produce enough tears to drown herself.

We didn't know these people and they didn't know us, but we instinctively knew they were a missionary family sending their fresh high school graduate to their home country for university. They probably wouldn't see their son for a couple of years. I don't know why, but missionary families know how to identify other missionary families, especially when they're saying heart-rending goodbyes. And this was definitely a missionary family releasing their third-culture kid into the vast unknown.

When Deborah tried to answer William's inquiry and explain why she was crying, she only managed a high-pitched cracking noise, but no discernible English words. This attempt at talking caused a new flood of tears to stream down her face. I started looking for a janitor with a mop.

William asked again, "Mom, are you okay? What's wrong?"

Eventually Deborah was able to find some words. Addressing William, James, Jonathan, me, God, the United Airlines desk agent, and the Japanese businessman in line behind us, she sobbed these words: "That boy just graduated from high school, and his parents are sending him overseas to college. And in just ten more years, William will graduate and leave, then in twelve years James will go, then in fourteen years it will be Jonathan. I don't think I can do this." More tears followed.

"So you're saying that being stuck with me is an unbearable thought." As usual, my attempt at diffusing the situation with sarcasm failed. The thought of being that far from her sons was not a happy one for my wife. Most parents send their eighteen-year-olds off to college, but few send them to the other side of the planet.

I'll never forget that airport scene. It seems like yesterday.

Some parents long for the day when all the kids are independent, grown up, out of their house, and off their budget. Not us (except the budget part). We wish we had a pause button so we could freeze a million different moments with our sons. Or maybe a rewind button so we could relive those million moments. Not because of guilt or regret, but just to enjoy them again exactly as they happened.

Ten years later, twelve years later, and fourteen years later, those dreaded moments happened. Our boys became men. They left. And we survived.

As I write this chapter, our sons are twenty-eight, twenty-six, and twenty-four. Two are married. One is a parent. We're grandparents. Life is good.

THE MOST AWKWARD INTRO EVER

One year after the crying-in-the-airport incident, I had an opportunity to minister at a church in a neighboring nation in Asia. It was my first time to preach in this church, and I was about to experience the most awkward introduction of my life.

"Our guest speaker tonight is Pastor Steve Murrell from the Philippines."

None of these church members knew me, and I didn't know them. My credibility (in their eyes) would soon be established by the way their beloved pastor introduced me. All they would know about me was what their pastor was about to tell them. Church people generally trust their pastor and distrust strangers, especially strangers with foreign accents. That's why the guest speaker introduction is so important. While the pastor introduced me, I sat on the front row, nervously shuffling my notes, and silently praying that God would help me honor Him and make disciples.

"Our guest speaker tonight is Pastor Steve Murrell from the Philippines. I'm going to have him come up here and introduce himself before he preaches."

What? Introduce myself?

I've introduced countless guest speakers at my church. I know how important the introduction is, and I'm pretty good at it. More than one guest preacher confessed that he would rather preach at my church than at his own, in part because of the way I introduce my guests. When I introduce a guest speaker at our church, I basically brag about him and his ministry.

If introducing is bragging, how should I introduce myself?

> Ladies and gentlemen, tonight, you have the privilege of learning from a great man. And, I have the great honor of introducing this great man to you. Besides leading the greatest church in the world, he is also the greatest living preacher. He is a great apostle, a great prophet, a great evangelist, a great pastor, and a really, really good teacher. Perhaps the greatest thing that can be said about this great man is that, in spite of all his greatness, he carries himself with great humility. Let's all rise to our feet and give a great standing ovation to the greatest guest speaker this church will ever have—me! Come on, you can clap louder than that.

Maybe a more humble approach, rooted in reality, would be better.

> Ladies and gentlemen, I have no idea why your pastor invited our guest speaker. Maybe no one else was available. Nevertheless, I was asked to introduce him tonight. He is nationally ignored and internationally unknown. He is the author of countless unwritten and unpublished imaginary bestsellers. After graduating without honors from Mississippi State University, this man led a tiny student church on the MSU campus that eventually shrunk and died. He took a few seminary courses, but never completed his theology degree. With this man and his ministry, when all is said and done, more is usually said than done. So, without further delay, let's stand to our feet and give an awkward, forced compulsory standing ovation to this complete stranger who is bragging about himself. Let's hear it for me!

I'm certain that introduction would have had them eating out of my hand. Here's how I actually introduced myself that night, as best as I can remember it.

JESUS IS THE STARTING POINT

Hi. I've never been asked to introduce myself before preaching. First of all, I'm a Christian and a cross-carrying, Bible-believing disciple of Christ. I'm here today because many years ago, as a sixteen-year-old high school student, I had a life-changing encounter with Jesus Christ that rearranged all my plans, dreams, priorities, and values. Since that day in 1975, He has been the central focus of my life. He is my Lord and my Master. He calls the shots.

That's the starting point. Who we are in Christ is who we are. I continued.

> Secondly, I'm a husband. My most sacred commitment, after my commitment to Jesus, is my commitment to my wife. She is my top priority after God. She is before my church and my ministry. She's more important to me than all the church members put together. God didn't call me to choose between a good marriage and a growing church, and He didn't call you to put success at work before success at home. Contrary to what many think, success at work and success at home are not mutually exclusive.

> Who we are in Christ is who we are.

How could I properly introduce myself without introducing my wife? We are one. Our lives are inexorably linked. Since Deborah was at home in Manila, I pulled out a recent photo of her from my Bible and passed it around the small church so everyone could see her.

Many years ago, before I was married, I heard a preacher say something about the importance of marriage and parenting that I hope I never forget. "If it doesn't work at home, don't export it."

Real Christianity is more than helping the poor, attending church, giving offerings, debating theology, and sleeping through sermons. We're in church meetings only a few hours each week. Real Christianity is twenty-four hours a day, seven days a week. It's easy to impress a crowd that only sees me for an hour on Sunday. What does it matter if I preach great sermons but can't be faithful to my wife?

Back to my introduction.

> Thirdly, I'm a father. I have three sons. William is nine. James is seven. Jonathan is five. My life calling is to honor God and make disciples, and my three young sons are my most important disciples. One day, they will either build up or tear down my life's work. I live for the day when, like Abraham, I lay my wrinkled hands on my children and grandchildren and pronounce a prophetic blessing. When it comes to my children, I try to think long-term. Everything I do is shaping their future. In fact, if my children are out of order, then I'm not even qualified to stand here and preach to you today.

At this point, my self-introduction was beginning to sound more like a sermon than a guest speaker introduction. I could see fear in their eyes. These people silently reasoned that if my introduction to myself was this long, the sermon itself would be at least an hour or two.

How God Measures Success

As my self-introduction continued, it meandered into a teaching from Genesis that is essential to understanding the heart of parenting. Modern Bible publishers divide Genesis into fifty chapters. The original writer created ten chapters or sections. Every time we read the phrase, "This is the account of" (NIV), it signals that a new section has begun.

A quick glance at some of these ten sections reveals God's view of success, legacy, parenting, and the next generation.

For instance, Genesis 11:27 says, "This is the account of Terah." After reading this statement, one would expect to read about Terah's life, his challenges, and his accomplishments. But surprisingly, only six verses are about Terah while thirteen chapters are about Terah's son, Abraham. The account of Terah is mostly about the next generation.

Likewise, Genesis 25:19 says, "This is the account of Abraham's son, Isaac." This time we get three verses about Isaac, followed by eleven chapters about his sons, Esau and Jacob.

This pattern is repeated in Genesis 37:2. "This is the account of Jacob." One verse about Jacob. One verse! Then we read fourteen chapters about his sons, primarily Joseph.

According to the pattern in Genesis, when God records the account of a person's life, He focuses primarily on what the next generation accomplishes. This tells me that if God were to write the account of Steve Murrell, He would include a comment or two about my life, followed by chapter after chapter after chapter about my sons, William, James, and Jonathan. The real and eternal account of my life will have little to do with how many churches I planted, how many people endured my sermons, how many people followed me on Twitter, or how many publishers accepted my manuscripts.

From God's perspective, the primary account of my life can only be measured long after I'm dead, as William, James, and Jonathan approach their finish lines. Therefore, it's never about my personal success. It's always about the next generation and setting them up for success.

God's perspective in Genesis is long-term and eternal, emphasizing truth and relationships. Our perspective is generally short-term and temporal, emphasizing cars, clothes, and other outward signs of popularity and material success.

THINGS THAT
MATTER MOST

Back to the longest self-introduction ever: "And finally, I'm a cross-cultural church planter and a pastor. A few years ago, my wife and I moved from Mississippi to the Philippines to start a church in Manila's University Belt."

This last point is where the typical guest preacher introduction begins and ends. Unfortunately, ministry success is often all that matters in the church world, just as financial success is all that matters in the business world. In many circles, it matters little if the guy is a good husband or father, as long as he is a good preacher. We don't care if our pastor's marriage is in trouble, as long as he can help us get through our troubles. We ignore the fact that his children are neglected and rebellious, as long as he can hire a good youth pastor to distract our kids from trouble. If it doesn't work at home, don't export it.

I'm serious about God's call on my life. He has called me to make disciples, develop leaders, and plant churches and campus ministries in every nation. It's my passion, my life work, and my job description. Fulfilling this mission is more important to me than money, security, comfort, and reputation. It's not more important than my wife and my sons. It can't happen apart from my family. In fact, it starts with my wife and my sons. My first and most important disciples are in my home. The most important place to develop leaders is in my home. If it does not work at home, don't export it.

I had one more part to my self-introduction that, like the rest, was totally made up on the spot.

> Oh yeah, I'm also a Little League T-ball coach. Our team, CitiBank, is 5-1 so far this season. James is our pitcher. Jonathan is our catcher. They are my two best hitters. William is playing second base for Apple Computers in the kid-pitch league.

This marked the end of my first and last self-introduction and the beginning of my sermon. I can't remember what I preached that day, but for some reason, I vividly remember the introduction where I basically laid out the priorities of my life. I outlined the things that matter most to me: Jesus, Deborah, William, James, Jonathan, Victory Manila (my church), and youth sports. In other words, I told them who I am. My identity begins with Christ. It includes my wife and children. It ends with my vocation and my hobbies.

PROPER PRIORITIES PROTECT THE SOUL

A young church planter recently asked me to help him with his sermon preparation skills, so we met at a coffee shop near my office. The more we talked about his sixty- to seventy-hour work week, the more I realized that sermon preparation was not the pressing issue in this man's life. Realizing his priorities were out of order, I began asking questions about his marriage and his four young children. His answers and his attempt to get the conversation back to sermon preparation confirmed to me that this dedicated young pastor was living on the edge of disaster regarding his family.

To help my friend see that his priorities needed major adjustments, I scribbled four words on the back of my Starbucks receipt: *Christian, husband, father, pastor.*

I pointed to these words on the receipt and emphatically declared, "This is *who* you are! *What* you do must flow from *who* you are."

I held the receipt up to his face and preached to him, "Because of who you are, there are four things you have to do: follow Jesus, love your wife, father your kids, lead your church."

Pointing to the list, I explained to my friend that no one can do the first three except him. If he does not do them, they won't happen. We can't hire staff to pray, read the Bible, and obey God for us. We can't delegate our relationship with our wife and kids. If we neglect these, they get neglected.

Number four is different. Leading the church can and should be staffed and delegated. In fact, the more church leadership is staffed and delegated, the more the church will grow in size, strength, and influence.

The first three — relationship with Jesus, relationship with spouse, relationship with kids — demands a one-man show. The last one — leading the church — demands a team.

I'm not sure if I helped my friend, but that hour in the coffee shop helped me. I always need to be reminded of who I am and what my priorities should be.

Jesus first. Deborah second. William, James, and Jonathan third. Victory and Every Nation fourth. Riding my motorcycle and scuba diving fifth and sixth.

A few days ago on my flight from Nashville to Manila, I was reading through Job and noticed that my self-introduction and my priorities seemed to mirror Job's introduction and priorities.

Notice how Job was introduced in Job 1:1-3.

In verse one, our first glimpse of Job tells us about his relationship with God. "There was a man in the land of Uz whose name was Job, and that man was blameless and upright, one who feared God and turned away from evil." Job is identified to readers as a man who was blameless, upright, and God-fearing. Our relationship with God should always be the starting point of our identity.

The second verse describes Job's family. "There were born to him seven sons and three daughters." After God, the next part of Job's introduction and the next relationship on his priority list was his family.

The third verse describes Job's career and his stuff. "He possessed 7,000 sheep, 3,000 camels, 500 yoke of oxen, and 500 female donkeys, and very many servants, so that this man was the greatest of all the people of the east." Sadly, many people's identities start and stop with their careers and their stuff. And sadder still, many preacher introductions and identities start and stop with ministry accomplishments and exaggerated numbers.

As we continue reading the book of Job, we find that Satan strikes Job's second and third priorities — his family and his possessions. Job loses everything except his relationship with God. In the middle of the most painful and seemingly unjust situation, watch how the Bible describes Job's response in Job 1:20. "Then Job arose and tore his robe and shaved his head and fell on the ground and worshiped."

If Job's family and his career or material possessions had been top priority and the core of his identity, he would not have responded this way to his loss. But because God was his center and the starting point of his identity, he responded with humility and worship (and a low-maintenance hairdo). "And he said, 'Naked I came from my mother's womb, and naked shall I return. The Lord gave, and the Lord has taken away; blessed be the name of the Lord'" (Job 1:21).

When the Lord is our first and our everything, even if we lose everything else (like Job), we will be able to bless the name of the Lord despite the pain we're experiencing. "In all this Job did not sin or charge God with wrong" (Job 1:22).

Here's my summary of verse three and of the life and times of Job: *No matter what goes wrong, God is never wrong, and He never wrongs us.* When he lost it all, Job didn't accuse God of wronging him. Rather, he worshiped God.

Having right priorities — God, family, stuff — protected Job's heart when disaster struck. While I'm sure the pain of losing family never left Job, in the end, God more than made up for what he lost. (See Job 42:10-17.) Proper priorities protected Job's heart in times of loss, and they will protect us when tough times hit hardest.

I Miss Those Days

About eleven years after that crying-in-the-airport experience, I was in seat 15C on a Southwest Airlines flight from Nashville to Houston. I couldn't help but notice a cute eighteen-month-old baby boy across the aisle in 15D. As I exchanged silly faces with this bald-headed baby, my mind filled with a collage of memories from decades past when our sons were little. I miss those days. At the time, our "baby" was a 180-pound sixteen-year-old budding artist and tennis champion.

On the next row in 14D, a frustrated father was wrestling with his energetic three-year-old girl who obviously wanted to run down the aisle while the seatbelt sign was on. Since she couldn't out-muscle dad, she decided to scream for the rest of the flight. I miss those days too. I really do.

> Proper priorities protected Job's heart in times of loss, and they will protect us when tough times hit hardest.

Why do they have to grow up so fast? Where is that pause button when we need it? They're born one day, and before you know it, they're graduating from college and getting married and *gone with the wind*.

Many of our friends have witnessed my wife when she spots a newborn baby, and it's the same scene every time. Whether we know the parents or not, Deborah will tell them how the first year was always "one of her favorite times" of parenting. Same thing happens when she sees a toddler. She declares that age to be her favorite. When she sees elementary school kids with lunch boxes and backpacks, she declares that to be one of her favorite seasons of life. Of course, teenage years are also her favorite, as well as college and adulthood.

I agree with her; they're all my favorites too. Seriously, Deborah and I thoroughly enjoyed every age and every stage of parenting. The ups, the downs, the good, the bad, the ugly—we loved it all. Always have. Always will. And we love being grandparents. Life keeps getting better and better.

> Love every moment of being a parent—the good moments and the bad moments, the laughing and the crying, the thrill of victory and the agony of defeat.

Like everything else in my life, the ultimate purpose of this book is to honor God and make disciples. The secondary purpose of this book is for my stories to help you love every moment of being a parent—the good moments and the bad moments, the laughing and the crying, the thrill of victory and the agony of defeat. Loving all of it, all the time, is my prayer for you.

NO-REGRET PARENTING

No-regret parenting is not the same as no-mistake parenting. I have made plenty of parental mistakes. I will address some of those mistakes in this book.

No matter my mistakes, I have no regrets for the time spent with my children. No regrets for the countless hours building Legos. No regrets for coaching so many Little League baseball games. No regrets for watching endless junior tennis tournaments in the brutal Manila heat. No regrets for leaving work early, fighting Manila's legendary traffic, only to be tortured by another piano recital. No regrets ever for time spent with my sons. And I have no regrets for the things I had to miss in order to spend time with my sons. And no regrets for the money spent to make those moments possible.

I'll finish this chapter with a recent example of what I mean by no-regret parenting. This story is so recent that it's still happening as I type these words. Last night was a short night and today will be a long and busy day. I'm already consuming my third cup of coffee, and I still feel like I have a caffeine deficiency. Here's what happened. I got to bed around two o'clock this morning knowing that I had to be at my office for an early eight o'clock international conference call with Every Nation regional leaders from Africa, Asia, Europe, Latin America, the Middle East, and North America.

I sacrificed sleep last night so I could drive three-and-a-half hours from Nashville to Memphis with my adult sons to watch the Memphis Grizzlies play basketball against the Golden State Warriors. These two teams currently have the best records in the NBA. We are Grizzlies fans, and we won in the last few seconds. Fortunately it didn't go into overtime, otherwise I would have slept even less.

As tired as I am today, I have no regrets about leaving work early yesterday to make the drive to Memphis with my sons. I have no regrets about spending money for gas, food, and game tickets. No regrets about spending almost another four hours in the car on the drive back home to Nashville.

Watching the game was great, but creating memories with my adult sons was even better.

One last thought as you consider the heart of parenting. The Bible teaches that life is short and fragile, like a breath, a shadow, and a mist. "Man is like a breath; his days are like a passing shadow" (Psalm 144:4). "What is your life? For you are a mist that appears for a little time and then vanishes" (James 4:14).

Before we know it, our kids are grown and gone. Therefore, as parents, we must seize the moment. Every moment. We must invest our all into being parents before the moment is "no more than a dream remembered, a Civilization gone with the wind."

DISCUSSION QUESTIONS

1. Did your parents prioritize family over work? If so, what actions demonstrated that to you and your siblings? If not, what actions demonstrated that to you and your siblings?

2. What is your biggest challenge in maintaining a healthy work/family balance? What can you do about it?

2

THE OLD MAN AND THE BOY
Lessons from My Father

When you are as old as the Old Man, you know a lot of things that you forgot you ever knew, because they've been a part of you so long.
Robert Ruark, *The Old Man and the Boy*

When the Old Man has an attack of philosophy coming on, all you can do is hold still and listen.
Robert Ruark, *The Old Man and the Boy*

Hear, O sons, a father's instruction, and be attentive, that you may gain insight . . .
Proverbs 4:1

I wish I had paid more attention to my dad when he was alive and had his occasional "attacks of philosophy." I'm sure I would be a better man today had I listened better then.

On January 28, 2002, at nine o'clock in the evening, my dad breathed his last breath and slipped from time into eternity. He was seventy-four years old. I was forty-two. He had been in and out of the hospital several times since 2001. His smoke-tortured lungs and rum-soaked liver just stopped working.

Dad died peacefully because he finally was at peace with God after a lifetime of disdaining preachers and resisting the gospel.

His journey to God hit warp speed when his heart stopped on October 11, 2001. The doctors were able to revive him, but more importantly, the Lord visited him. While laying on his back in the emergency room, he came face-to-face with the God of eternity and lived to tell about it.

In fact, he later told my younger brother that when his heart stopped, he had a vision that he left his body and came face-to-face with Jesus, who was giving him one last chance. In the vision, as he watched the doctors frantically try to revive him, he suddenly saw a whiskey bottle, a pack of cigarettes, a gun, and a Bible floating around his lifeless body in the emergency room. He knew he had a choice to make.

He later told my brother that, in that moment, he decided to choose the Bible rather than the things that were destroying his life. As soon as he chose the Bible, his vision was over, his heart started beating, and he was back in his body, eyes wide open, staring at the doctors who were congratulating themselves on reviving him. He was never the same after that experience.

DAD'S FUNERAL

Three months later, he would face God again, this time forever. But he was ready.

I was in New York City visiting our new Every Nation church when my brother called, saying that I should get on the next plane to Mississippi if I wanted to see my dad alive. While on the plane, I wrote what would be my last words to Dad. I recited them at his bedside and read them at his funeral a few days later.

Here's what I wrote on that sad flight:

> Thanks, Dad, for never missing a baseball game, basketball game, football game, track meet, birthday party, or anything else that mattered as I was growing up.

> Thanks for always being there for me every time I crossed the finish line at a high school track meet, when I fell through the frozen lake while duck hunting when I was nine, that time Mike Croswell's easy grounder rolled under my glove at second base (costing us the Little League championship).

> You were always there for me, and I'm glad the Lord allowed me to be there with you when you crossed your final finish line.

> Thanks for trusting me and supporting me, especially when I: grew long hair in the seventies, quit the football team in tenth grade, became a pastor rather than your business partner, moved to the other side of the world to be a missionary.

> Thanks for teaching me to: ride a bike and drive a car, throw a baseball and hit a golf ball, fly fish and quail hunt, work hard and save money, write a check and pick a mutual fund.

> Thank you for teaching me to be a real boy and a real man, to be a good son and a good father.

A day after the funeral, I gathered with my brothers and sisters to discuss Dad's will, which, like every business matter in his life, was meticulously detailed. As expected, all five kids inherited equal shares of cash and real estate.

MY MOST-TREASURED INHERITANCE

Two items were not specifically willed to me, but I wanted them. Fortunately, my siblings were agreeable and let me have Dad's 1959 Rolex and an original copy of his favorite book, *The Old Man and the Boy* by Robert Ruark.

Dad was a voracious reader and our house was filled with books, but he had said many times that this book was his favorite. I had never read *The Old Man and the Boy*, but I had to have this well-worn hardback. Somehow I instinctively knew that it would connect me to my father long after he was dead and gone.

The 1959 Rolex found a home among my small watch collection in my safe. *The Old Man and the Boy* took its place on my bookshelf. For years I never wore the Rolex and never read the book, but they were among my most-treasured possessions.

When I finally got around to reading *The Old Man and the Boy*, suddenly my dad's fathering strategy made sense to me. I understood the kind of dad he was trying to be for my brothers and me. (I'm not so sure his hunting, fishing, and sports-focused fathering methodology really connected with my sisters.) The book made me appreciate him and miss him more than ever. And I think it helped me become a better father to my three sons.

The Old Man and the Boy originally appeared as a series of stories Ruark wrote for *Field & Stream* magazine from 1953 through 1961. Eventually, some of these stories were expanded, edited, and published as a semi-autobiographical novel, also entitled *The Old Man and the Boy*. The magazine stories and book feature young Bobby and his grandfather, the Old Man, whose ultimate goal was to help the young boy become a man.

The Old Man teaches Bobby to hunt and fish, be a gentleman and a sportsman, enjoy nature and love books, and value education and protect the environment. Every hunting and fishing story carries a life lesson that is vital to Bobby becoming a man.

Reading the book reminded me of the list I read at Dad's funeral. Yeah, I'm pretty sure Dad patterned his parenting after the Old Man in the book. And I'm glad he did.

By the time Bobby is in high school, the Old Man is dying. But before he dies, he tells Bobby that he's proud of him. Every young man needs to hear "I am proud of you" from a father figure. Some people believe that a boy can never really become a man until a father figure affirms him with such pride. Bobby takes the Old Man's life lessons with him to the battlefields of World War II, to post-war African safaris, and on Atlantic fishing adventures.

Every time I read *The Old Man and the Boy*, I realize what Dad was trying to do as a father, and my eyes sweat. Maybe I should explain sweaty eyes. When I was about six years old, I busted my lip wrestling my big brother at our family farm about thirty miles from our home in Jackson, Mississippi. With blood and tears all over my face, my tough West Texas dad told me that real men don't cry. At six, I'm not sure I was a real man, but the tears immediately stopped, though the blood didn't. I have not cried since, but occasionally my eyes sweat. They seem to sweat every time I read a chapter in *The Old Man and the Boy*.

Looking back, I'm sure many of the lessons my dad tried to teach me were lessons he learned from the Old Man in the book. As a young boy, many of Dad's life lessons were lost on me. Back then, he often seemed unfair or too tough. Now I get it. His ultimate goal was not my momentary childhood happiness, but my long-term manhood. Like the Old Man in the book, everything Dad did was to prepare me for an honorable manhood.

Six Life Lessons From My Father

Here are five of those six life lessons Dad attempted to teach me. Some of them I learned as soon as they were taught. Others have taken me a lifetime to understand and incorporate into my life. I did my best to teach these lessons to my sons.

1. Hard Work Versus Entitlement

Several years ago, Deborah and I hosted an American pastor in our Manila apartment. After a couple days of trying to keep up with my schedule, he commented, "You sure are working hard." His observation was accurate. I do work hard. I've worked hard my whole life. I have my dad to thank for my obsessive work ethic.

Dad was old-school. He felt it was his parental duty to teach the next generation the value of minimum-wage, back-breaking, manual labor. He could find no good reason an able-bodied teenager was not working in the summer.

The first job my dad arranged for me was digging ditches. That's right. When I was fifteen, my dad secured summer jobs for my brother and me as ditch-diggers, installing underground telephone cables ten hours a day in the 100°F Mississippi heat for $2.10 an hour.

Since I complained so much about the heat, the next summer, he got me an indoor job. So I spent the summer of 1976 inside an *un*-air-conditioned warehouse loading fifty-pound fertilizer bags onto pallets and into eighteen-wheel tractor-trailers. During our breaks, we would go outside to the brutal Southern summer heat and humidity to cool off. The inside of that warehouse was hotter than outside.

The aforementioned fond summer memories flashed into my head this morning as I read Proverbs 12:11, "Whoever works his land will have plenty of bread, but he who follows worthless pursuits lacks sense."

My dad wasn't very religious, so I doubt he ever read that Bible verse, but he sure taught the principle. I learned from the Bible and my dad that abundance and work are connected. People don't seem to get the concept of hard work anymore. They want instant success, promotion, prosperity, church growth, whatever — without actually working. I know fresh college graduates who don't understand why the CEO has perks that aren't available to them. They say, "Aren't we all created equal?" Sorry, but life doesn't work that way. In the real world, participation trophies don't exist, the score is kept, and some teams actually lose.

Fantasies and work aren't connected. It's a simple choice: work or chase fantasies. We can't do both. How many business people chase easy-money fantasies, while refusing to do the hard work required for success? I've lost count of kids with athletic "potential" who never make it because they're simply too lazy to succeed. And I've watched too many church planters chase fantasy strategies that produce nothing but phantom disciples, while refusing to put in the hard work required to make actual disciples.

I fear that many Christians are confused about grace and work. These concepts are not mutually exclusive. In fact, they're both essential in any and every career. And they're also essential to parenting.

Notice how the apostle Paul embraced both grace and hard work. "But by the grace of God I am what I am, and his grace toward me was not in vain. On the contrary, I worked harder than any of them, though it was not I, but the grace of God that is with me" (1 Corinthians 15:10).

Paul's response to God's grace was that he "worked harder than any of them." Paul's understanding of God's grace did not allow him to do nothing and use grace as a divine excuse for laziness. Paul acknowledged that his hard work was empowered by God's grace. He said the reason for his hard work was, "not I, but the grace of God."

I'm thankful for a dad who taught me the value of hard work. Learning from our parents and grandparents, Deborah and I were determined to raise sons who understood and embraced an old-school work ethic. Whether on the tennis courts, basketball court, piano bench, or in the classroom, Deborah and I expected our sons to give effort that was wholehearted, energetic, one hundred percent, all-or-nothing. Laziness and the *pwede na* ("good enough already") attitude were never tolerated in our family.

2. Saving Versus Spending

A few hundred years ago, John Wesley encouraged his disciples to "earn all you can, save all you can, and give all you can." My dad had probably not read any of Wesley's books, but I am sure he would agree with Wesley's conservative view of work, money, and saving.

I'm forever grateful for a dad who taught me to work, save, invest, and wait patiently for success. Over the years, I've watched so many friends get tricked into get-rich-quick traps that seem so obviously foolish to me, but not to them. I'm sure I'm able to discern unwise money schemes because of the foundation my dad put in my life.

> I fear that many Christians are confused about grace and work. These concepts are not mutually exclusive. In fact, they're both essential in any and every career.

When they were old enough to count, before they could read or write, Deborah and I started teaching our sons how to manage God's money. Each of them had four cups with the following labels: offering, gifts, saving, spending. They put one-fourth of their money in each cup. The first twenty-five percent was given at church as the tithe, mission offerings, or to the poor. (Yes, the tithe is technically a tenth, not a fourth, but it was easier for them to simply divide their money into four equal parts.) Our goal was to teach them the joy of giving and the wisdom of saving. This four-cup banking system did the trick.

The next twenty-five percent was for buying birthday and Christmas gifts for friends and family. Of course, we always supplemented this fund and helped them purchase gifts for their friends. The third twenty-five percent was for saving. And the final twenty-five percent could be spent however they wanted. More often than not, they discussed those expenditures with us. As they grew older, they stopped using the four cups, but they continued giving offerings to their church, missions, and the poor. They also continued to save and invest. When it comes to money management, we have found Proverbs 22:6 to be true: "Train up a child in the way he should go; even when he is old he will not depart from it."

> We decided we didn't want to be a television family. We preferred to be a music, sports, and book family.

3. Outdoors Versus Indoors

Like the Old Man in the book, my dad taught his five children to love the outdoors by example. Hunting, fishing, golf, baseball, football, water skiing, yard work, farming, gardening, and horseback riding were all part of our lives growing up. I must confess that today, I hate some of the activities on this list—especially golf, gardening, and all forms of yard work. Nevertheless, I'm glad I was raised outside. We weren't much of a TV or movie family. We actually did stuff, rather than watching others do stuff. We did reality, rather than watching reality shows. We got dirty, sweaty, and bloody. We fell off horses, broke bones, got stitches, and lived to tell about it. I'm thankful my parents didn't allow us to grow up staring at a screen. They made us go outside and play until they told us to come inside or until someone got too hurt to continue.

When our sons were young, we didn't have a television. Not because of a religious conviction, and not because we were poor missionaries who could not afford one. We decided we didn't want to be a television family. We preferred to be a music, sports, and book family. And we actually talked to each other for extended periods of time.

The downside of not being a screen-centered family is that today, as adults, my sons are terrible at video games. By not allowing them to spend countless hours in front of video game consoles during their formative years, we scarred them for life and deprived them of important gaming skills they'll probably never be able to acquire. I hope they'll forgive us one day for this deficit, and I trust that by the grace of God, they'll become functional adults despite their lack of video game skills.

Eventually, we purchased a television, but we only used it to play VHS tapes. (If you don't know what a VHS tape is, ask your grandparents.) Then, in the summer of 2000, we joined the human race and got cable so we could watch the Sydney Summer Olympics. Now we're normal.

I'm grateful that my parents raised me to be an outdoor kid, and I'm thankful that despite growing up in a concrete jungle, my sons love the outdoors.

4. Entrepreneurship Versus Employment

My dad often exhorted my two brothers, my two sisters, and me to never get jobs, but to start a business or businesses. He wanted us to be our own bosses and create jobs for others. I'm sure that's part of why I became a serial entrepreneurial church planter, rather than a mainline pastor working for one church or a traditional missionary working for a mission agency. I think I've successfully passed that entrepreneurial value to two of my sons, who are well on their way to being serial entrepreneurs.

Along with making more money, a big part of my dad's motivation for creating his own business and being his own boss was that he could control his own schedule. Controlling his schedule enabled him to attend all his kids' sporting events and other family activities. It also allowed him to get to the golf course and go hunting and fishing when necessary.

When some of my Chinese-Filipino friends first heard me explain my dad's entrepreneurial ideas, they asked me if he was part-Chinese. I told them, "Yes, he was West Texas Chinese."

5. Trust Versus Micromanagement

One of the best parenting examples my parents set for me was to trust my siblings and me, even when we didn't deserve their trust. They believed in us, even when they should have doubted. I had freedom when many of my friends were micromanaged. No matter what I did, I always knew my parents had my back. Win or lose, they were my biggest fans. Maybe if they had micromanaged us more, we would have had fewer stitches, broken bones, and hospital visits. But we also would have missed many of the life experiences that formed us into the functional adults we became.

Deborah and I have never regretted trusting our sons. We have, at times, regretted micromanaging them.

Obviously, the younger they are, the more we must micromanage them just to keep them alive. We put up gates and fences to keep them from falling down stairs or running in streets. We completely control what and when they eat. We decide what they wear and when they go to bed. We totally micromanage babies and toddlers, and we should. I silently laugh and invisibly shake my head when I hear new parents attempting to reason with their toddler, offering them choices rather than telling them what to do like functional adults have done for thousands of years.

As our children grow up, we micromanage and control them less and less.

When my sons were teen-agers, Deborah and I tried to figure out how much we should or could control them. Our different views of parental control came

> Deborah and I have never regretted trusting our sons. We have, at times, regretted micromanaging them.

to a humorous head one weekend when the boys planned a camping trip to Corregidor Island with some friends.

With tents, sleeping bags, camp food, and backpacks prepared, Deborah's last words as they left our Manila apartment were, "Have fun and be careful. Don't do anything dangerous. I love you."

My parting words were, "Have fun and be fearless. Climb a mountain and jump off a cliff (into the ocean). I love you."

I guess this explains why kids need a father and a mother. One to push them out of their comfort zones and one to protect them from youthful craziness; one to challenge them and one to comfort them. Fact is, I don't think they really listened to either of us that day. And they had a blast jumping off Corregidor's cliffs into the South China Sea. They returned home with a few scratches and scrapes and, more importantly, with some great adventure stories and lifelong memories.

My Most Painful
Life Lesson

I learned one final lesson, not from my dad, but because of my dad. It was by far the most difficult lesson of my life. In fact, I have had to learn and relearn it over and over almost every day of my life.

6. Forgiveness

Sounds simple enough, but in my case, this lesson has taken a lifetime to learn and apply. Every time I think I've finally fully forgiven, another memory emerges, and I get another opportunity to forgive my well-meaning, but flawed, dad.

For example, when I started coaching my sons in Little League T-ball, painful memories of my dad coaching my teams began to torment my mind, and I again had a choice to forgive or nurture bitterness.

Little League baseball is a good snapshot of the best and worst of my dad and my childhood. My best friends were my team-mates. My mom was team mom. My big brother was my hero and the team superstar. And my dad was my coach. I loved watching, practicing, and playing Little League baseball.

Except when we had a night game. Then it was a nightmare. If we had an early game, it was great. But those night games were a different story.

Though he would never admit it, my dad, like his dad, was an alcoholic. Dad was not one of those jolly, happy drunks like in the movies. Alcohol made him mean. Never physically violent, but he elevated verbal violence to an art form. When inebriated, he was the Rembrandt of verbal abuse.

My eyes are sweating now as I remember my intoxicated dad "coaching" my night games way back in the summer of 1969. The humiliation mixed with anger feels as real today as four decades ago. And again, I make a decision to forgive, let it go, and remember and celebrate the good times.

Of all the life lessons from my dad, maybe forgiveness is the most important. I've been forgiven so much by my heavenly Father, how dare I not forgive my earthly father?

Forgiveness is at the heart of parenting. Forgiving my parents, especially my dad. Forgiving my children. Teaching my children to forgive me. And most importantly, receiving forgiveness from God, and teaching my sons to receive His forgiveness.

DISCUSSION QUESTIONS

1. What are the most important lessons you learned from your parents?

2. What are some things you have had to learn to forgive your parents for doing?

3

A TALE OF TWO CITIES
Doing Family in Manila and Nashville

It was the best of times, it was the worst of times . . .
it was the season of Light, it was the season of
Darkness, it was the spring of hope, it was the
winter of despair, we had everything before us, we
had nothing before us . . .
Charles Dickens, *A Tale of Two Cities*

But our citizenship is in heaven, and from it we
await a Savior, the Lord Jesus Christ . . .
Philippians 3:20

If they had been thinking of that land from
which they had gone out, they would have had
opportunity to return.
Hebrews 11:15

After living in Manila for twenty-four years, for the
past eight years, Deborah and I have been splitting
time between Manila, Nashville, and Delta Airlines.
Our lives often feel like a tale of two cities (or maybe
two airports).

Doing life and family in Asia and then in America has been
the best of times and the worst of times, all at the same time.

Sometimes it seemed like we got the best of both worlds — the best of Filipino culture and the best of American culture. Sometimes I'm afraid we've experienced the worst of both.

In our two cities and in our two lives, we have lived what Charles Dickens calls "the epoch of belief and the epoch of incredulity, the season of light and the season of darkness, the spring of hope and the winter of despair." And we would do it all over again, without changing a thing, if given a choice.

In chapter one, I told a story of Deborah getting a bit emotional at the Manila airport as we watched a missionary family saying goodbye to their son who was moving overseas for college. Eventually, we experienced that same tearful "season of darkness" and "winter of despair" mixed with a bit of separation anxiety as our sons became adults on the other side of the ocean.

William, James, and Jonathan were all born at Makati Medical Center in the Philippines and raised in Metro Manila. They attended elementary and high school in Antipolo, and eventually moved to Nashville to study, play college tennis, and find daughters-in-law for Deborah and me. William and James competed and studied at Lipscomb University. Jonathan chose a cross-town rival, Belmont University. All three graduated with Latin words after their names. Deborah and I are proud of our sons, and thankful for them. We are also thankful that we got to raise them overseas in a different world than the one we grew up in.

My three sons are American citizens, without an American worldview. William, James, and Jonathan are what missiologists, sociologists, and anthropologists call "third-culture kids."

Of course, William's first job after college graduation was in a little farming community in Normandy, France. After a year in France, he decided to get a master's degree in Oxford, England. It made perfect sense. An American kid born and raised in Asia, university studies in the USA, first job in France, then graduate studies in England. It made sense because our sons were raised as third-culture kids.

RAISING THIRD-CULTURE KIDS

Here's the simplest way I can describe third-culture families that raise third-culture kids. Sometimes when we say we're "going home," we mean Manila, and sometimes we mean Nashville. Being a third-culture family also means we don't feel totally at home in either of our home cities. In Nashville, we miss festive Filipino culture, our Filipino church (Victory Manila), and our Filipino friends. In Manila, we miss orderly American culture, our American church (Bethel), and our American friends.

Here are a couple of stories that might help explain third-culture people.

Ten years ago, William was being recruited to play tennis at Lipscomb University. We were in Manila. He was in Nashville. Our phone call with him went something like this.

Me: "How'd you like the Lipscomb campus tour?"

William: "Nashville's a cool city. I love the campus. Coach seems like a good guy. And they have plans to build a new tennis center."

Me: "That sounds great. You think you'll accept their offer?"

William: "I don't know."

Me: "Why?"

William: "I've never been around so many white people in my life. I'm not sure I'll fit in."

Me: "Son, you might want to look in the mirror every now and then."

Growing up as a white kid in a brown world, it took a while for William to get used to living in a white-majority culture.

After visiting a few other schools, William eventually decided to enroll at Lipscomb. Eighteen months later, a broken ankle ended his athletic career and opened the door for his academic career. But that's a different story about the sovereignty of God.

A few years after William's first visit to Lipscomb, we were in Nashville having a meal with the family. James had followed his brother to Lipscomb, and he was telling us about his most recent third-culture experience in America. That week, his business ethics class was discussing and debating real case studies and the moral and ethical implications of moving manufacturing jobs overseas where labor costs were cheaper.

It soon became evident that every student in the class took the same side of the argument—except for James. Even the professor seemed to be on the other side. But by the time James made his case and defended his position, about half the class agreed with him. Even the professor seemed to be convinced.

The case study was about a Tennessee factory that was closing its local operation and moving to Vietnam. One hundred American jobs would be lost. But 300 Vietnamese jobs would be created, lowering manufacturing costs and increasing company profits in the process.

Every student in the class, except for James, argued that it was unethical to deprive hardworking Americans of their jobs, even if it created three times as many jobs for poorer families overseas. Furthermore, they unanimously agreed that it was morally wrong to "exploit" poor Vietnamese workers in order to lower manufacturing costs. Some students even argued that if the company moved the jobs to Vietnam, the owners were ethically obligated to pay the same wages they paid their American workers.

James didn't agree with any of the points his classmates made. He won the argument and half of the class to his side by asking a few questions that no one wanted to answer. Here's what James asked: "Why is it more ethical to provide one hundred jobs in Tennessee than 300 jobs in Vietnam? Why are one hundred American families more valuable and deserving of work than 300 Vietnamese families?"

James had a completely different perspective than everyone else in his class because he was born and raised in a developing nation as a third-culture kid. The fact that he lived most of his life in a city filled with urban poor shaped how he views the world and how he discerns what is and isn't ethical. It's not something he can turn on and off. It's the lens through which he constantly sees the world every day.

> In some way, we're all supposed to raise third–culture kids. As Kingdom–first kids, they belong to two cultures: the culture of their birth and the culture of God's Kingdom.

Because of where he was raised, where he went to school, where he went to church, where he played basketball, and the fact that he played *patintero* (a Filipino game played on the street), James had a different under-standing of and sensitivity to the poor than most of his classmates. From his perspective, poor Asians are no less valuable and no less deserving of jobs than poor Americans. He appreciates his American passport, but he will never think exclusively like an American.

Jonathan eventually followed his brothers to Nashville to play tennis and get a degree (which apparently doesn't always require attending class and studying). He chose Belmont rather than Lipscomb, partly because the Lipscomb tennis team was made up of all American white guys, while the Belmont team was all brown Brazilians. Jonathan was the only white American on the Belmont team. To him, his Brazilian teammates looked and acted more like his Filipino friends. Don't get me wrong, Jonathan has nothing against white Americans. But like all third–culture individuals, he prefers diversity to uniformity.

THE BEST OF BOTH WORLDS

Like many third-culture kids, my sons can be described as white on the outside and brown on the inside. They have American passports, Philippine birth certificates, and Philippine yellow cards (a.k.a. permanent resident visas). They look like Americans, but sometimes they think, act, and eat like Filipinos. But, compared to their real Filipino friends, they aren't Filipino at all and never will be. And I'm not sure they'll ever really think or act like Americans either.

Raised as third-culture kids, today they are third-culture adults, and will be for the rest of their lives. In the process, Deborah and I also gradually became third-culture adults. We see the world differently than our Filipino and American friends.

Deborah and I often thank God for the privilege of raising our kids in the Philippines. We're convinced that their global perspective will give them a huge advantage, no matter what careers they choose. We like to think that they got the best of both worlds.

In some way, we're all supposed to raise third-culture kids—not fully American, Filipino, Japanese, Nigerian, or British, but Kingdom-first kids. As Kingdom-first kids, they belong to two cultures: the culture of their birth and the culture of God's Kingdom.

Every culture includes values that reflect the glory and image of God, and every culture has values that are fallen and broken. In chapter two, I introduced five American cultural values that my dad instilled in my siblings and me. But I added a sixth, forgiveness, that transcends all cultures. I tried my best to teach all six to my sons. Since they didn't grow up in an American culture, I'm not sure those original five values were planted as deeply in them as my dad planted them in me, but at least they're there in seed form.

Before I introduce you to five Filipino cultural values that helped Deborah and me develop character in our sons, I need to explain a few cultural disclaimers.

First, we need to recognize that every culture is a mixture of godly and not-so-godly values. No culture is purely godly and none is purely evil. They are all a mixture. Deborah and I have tried to embrace the godly parts of the American culture that shaped us and the godly parts of the Filipino culture that helped shape our sons. Likewise, we have tried to discern and reject the parts that don't honor God. We tried to use both American and Filipino influences to help them become the men God designed them to be. Embracing the godly side of these five Filipino cultural traits, along with the best of our American culture, helped us give our sons the best of both worlds. These five traits are a core part of Filipino culture, but they are also Kingdom traits that would be good to impart to any and all kids, regardless of nationality. And like all cultural influences, they have a negative side as well as a positive side.

And that brings me to my second disclaimer. Every cultural value has a dark side that we would do well to identify and avoid. If you are familiar with the *StrengthsFinder* books and tests, you know that each "strength" or "theme" also has a corresponding weakness. For example, people who have communication as a strength can sometimes over-communicate when they should simply listen (thus their strength becomes a weakness). People who have harmony as a strength are usually good peacemakers, but often are not so good at confrontation. Their desire for harmony can cloud the need for temporary conflict that's often necessary for lasting harmony. People who have command can become controlling. The list goes on and on. Every strength or theme is a two-sided coin with a strength on one side and a weakness on the other side. The trick is to recognize and develop our strengths, while simultaneously tempering them so we don't become cartoonish caricatures of ourselves.

My final disclaimer is that all cultures have a bit of overlap. As I will point out in upcoming paragraphs, all cultures have some type of family value. Some place family cultural values at the top of the list, others allow it to slip under career or individuality, but they all place some value on family. In chapter two, I wrote about how my dad taught me to have a strong work ethic. The idea of hard work is not unique to America, but Americans tend to take it to the extreme compared to many other cultures. Likewise, gratitude and honor are core parts of many cultures, but the role they play in the daily life of Filipinos certainly helped us impart those values to our kids.

Having presented my disclaimers, here's the opinion of one expat (me), on how the positive side of a few Filipino cultural values helped my third-culture kids become productive, God-honoring, third-culture adults.

1. *Utang na loob* (debt of gratitude)

Before William could walk or talk, we realized that we couldn't teach our kids everything, so we made a short list of what we had to teach them. At the top of our list was gratitude. We had no interest in adding three more kids to the millions of self-absorbed, entitled brats. Raising our sons in a world of *utang na loob* made this task a little easier than it would have been in another culture.

As a foreigner, I'm not sure I will ever fully understand *utang na loob* or be able to adequately explain it, but I have experienced the positive manifestation of this pillar of Filipino culture for thirty-two years.

Utang na loob literally means "debt of inside." It transliterates as "a debt of one's inner self." It's often translated as "debt of gratitude." I don't know if this is linguistically true, but from my foreign perspective, it seems that Filipinos gain two positive traits from the debt-of-gratitude culture: life-long loyalty and sacrificial generosity. The catch is that relational loyalty and radical generosity are primarily extended to people who are perceived to be owed a deep debt. *Utang na loob* can be relationally manipulative if it's demanded, but it can also be a powerful relational force when it's freely given because of real gratitude.

As with all cultural strengths and themes, there is certainly a perverse side to *utang na loob*, but I'm only dealing with cultural positives in this chapter. From my Western perspective, the positive side of *utang na loob* is the desire to attempt to repay a person for a favor given. The problem occurs when that favor is unquantifiable, making the repayment extremely elusive. On the other hand, when money is loaned, we know exactly how much is owed and exactly when it has been fully repaid, so we reach a point of no more debt. *Utang na loob* typically deals with invisible relational debt that can never fully be quantified or repaid.

In the thirty-two years since Deborah and I landed in Manila for a never-ending "one month" summer mission trip in 1984, I've often felt over-honored and over-appreciated. Sometimes the honor extended to me has made me feel uncomfortable; other times it has humbled or confused me. I've grown to realize that the over-honor and extreme gratefulness is not so much about me and what I did; it's about *utang na loob* and a debt of gratitude that has been planted deep in the souls of Filipinos for generations.

For instance, about eighteen years ago when my longtime next-door neighbor, Joey Bonifacio, decided to air-condition his home, he also air-conditioned my home. He spent thousands of dollars and called it a birthday gift, even though my birthday was six months away. Joey's now adult son Joseph recently told me that when he was a little boy, his dad gathered their three young sons together and explained that he was buying the Murrells air conditioners. Joey's explanation was: "I don't know where my marriage would be today, and I don't know what kind of father I would be today, if Steve and Deborah had not come to our nation." That was *utang na loob* in Joey's heart motivating his gratefulness and his extremely generous gift to my family. It was not me hinting that I was owed something or that our house was brutally hot in Manila's summer. Joey owed me nothing. In fact, Joey's constant extreme generosity often made me feel very uncomfortable. He is one of those friends "who sticks closer than a brother" that Proverbs 18:24 describes. And maybe that kind of friendship is also rooted in the good and godly side of *utang na loob*.

I recently tried to explain this concept to a Western pastor who asked me why the Filipinos in my Manila church are so loyal to me and the Filipinos in his American church don't seem to be loyal at all. I said their loyalty to me wasn't because of anything I had done, but because of *utang na loob* — a debt of gratitude — inside of them. I then explained to my friend that I'm equally loyal to them for the same reason. They feel like they owe me. I feel like I owe them. I expect this mutual feeling of gratitude to last a lifetime. After thirty-two years, my sense of debt to my Filipino friends seems to only get stronger as if I've paid none of it off and compound (relational) interest has grown exponentially out of control. But the funny thing is, they don't think I owe them anything and I don't think they owe me anything. It's just the way their world works.

> Being immersed in a culture rooted in *utang na loob* helped Deborah and me plant the seeds of gratitude, humility, community, and relational loyalty deep in the hearts of our sons.

I explained to my American pastor friend that *utang na loob* is a lot like the advice of the wise old men that Rehoboam foolishly rejected in 1 Kings 12:7, "If you will be a servant to this people today and serve them, and speak good words to them when you answer them, then they will be your servants forever."

I told my friend that if he would befriend and serve the Filipinos in his church, they would be his loyal friends forever. I hope he listened.

Two verses come to mind when I attempt to explain *utang na loob*. Both describe the fruit and the end result of this powerful cultural force. Proverbs 18:24 says that, "A man of many companions may come to ruin, but there is a friend who sticks closer than a brother." And in Proverbs 17:17, we read, "A friend loves at all times, and a brother is born for adversity."

Deborah and I were determined to raise grateful kids. I'm sure we would have made this a top priority no matter where we lived. But raising our sons in a culture where relational gratitude is viewed as a debt that can never be completely repaid helped reinforce what we wanted to teach them. Being immersed in a culture rooted in *utang na loob* helped Deborah and me plant the seeds of gratitude, humility, community, and relational loyalty deep in the hearts of our sons.

We tried our best to instill in our sons the importance of finding and being the type of friend who sticks "closer than a brother," who "loves at all times," and who is "born for adversity."

Of course the best example of *utang ng loob* is the gospel. Jesus did something for us, and we are forever grateful. Out of this gratefulness, we will do anything for Him, and we will be loyal to Him for life. In short, we owe Him everything.

2. *Pamilya* (family)

At some level, family values are found in all societies, but Filipino culture seems to take family to another level — sometimes in a healthy way, sometimes not so much. It's difficult to explain to an outsider the importance of family, including extended family, in Filipino culture. Family is first, second, third, and fourth on the priority list.

Like gratitude, I'm sure Deborah and I would have taught our sons the value of family no matter where we lived. But living in a family-first society made our job that much easier.

Here's an example of how Filipinos see family. Unlike many Westerners, Filipinos would never consider sending aging parents or grandparents to a nursing home. When the elderly are unable to live alone, adult sons and daughters automatically take them into their homes and provide care for life, whether they can afford it or not. *Utang ng loob* in action. Of course this isn't unique to Filipino culture. Most families in the Southern hemisphere and Middle East function the same way.

Foundational to the *pamilya* value is respect and honor extended to elders. This is the fruit of centuries of Filipino Catholicism that taught the biblical principle of honoring father and mother. In the Filipino world, honor and respect starts with parents and grandparents and extends to older siblings, as well as other elders who may or may not actually be relatives. It took me quite a while to get used to hearing *po* (untranslatable, but close to "sir") from students and church members who were not much younger than me. It always made me feel old.

Because of so many strong Filipino families in our church community, our kids were influenced by the healthy part of Filipino *pamilya*, and for that I owe my Filipino friends a debt of gratitude that I can never repay.

Unlike my wife, I didn't grow up around extended family. Spending most of my adult life in the Philippines gave me an up-close-and-personal view of the power of extended families.

We certainly didn't do everything right, but in retrospect, I think we got this one right. If you asked my sons today, I think they would tell you that they never felt that our ministry was more important to us than our family. They were first, and they knew it.

3. *Paggalang* (respect for elders)

From their very first words, Filipino kids are taught to show verbal respect to anyone who is older than them. My Filipino friend Carlos used to work in a Manila call center, training Filipinos to deal with Western clients. One of his most difficult tasks was getting them to stop saying "Sir" and "Ma'am" constantly. After several female clients complained that being addressed as "Ma'am" was an insult because they were not old women, the American call center manager instructed Carlos to train the Filipinos to stop saying "Sir" and "Ma'am." Carlos admits that he never fully succeeded in getting most of his Filipino trainees to drop the verbal titles of respect. Verbal respect and honor are just too deep in the Filipino soul.

This culture of respect and honor is very similar to the West Texas values I learned from my dad and the Southern values Deborah learned from her parents. We said, "Yes, Sir" and "No, Sir." "Yes, Ma'am" and "No, Ma'am." We were taught to say "Mister" and "Misses" to people who were older than us. Today I'm fifty-five, and I still say "Sir" and "Ma'am" to people who are my parents' age. It's that deep in me.

We were going to teach our sons to use verbal respect vocabulary no matter where they were raised. The fact that everyone around them also expressed verbal respect to elders made our job that much easier.

Eventually, my sons learned the Western athletic value of trash-talking, but it took a while to take root in their *paggalang*-influenced vocabulary. I hope this value of verbal respect is so deep in them that, like those call center trainees, they will have a hard time dropping the language of respect and honor even if the culture around them is rooted in disrespect.

4. *Edukasyon* (education)

As many times as I had heard that Filipinos value education and learning, I didn't understand how much until my first visit to a provincial Filipino home. Deborah and I had been living in the Philippines for a couple of years, but we had never visited any of the 7,000 Philippine Islands besides the one we lived on—Luzon. We were planting a new church in Iloilo, the hometown of one of Victory's first pastors, Jun Escosar. Iloilo is on the island of Panay in the central Philippines, a ninety-minute flight from Manila.

When I met Jun in 1984 at an early outreach in Manila, he was a skinny student fresh from the province. Of course, thirty years later, because of the way Filipinos value *edukasyon*, Jun is now Dr. Anastacio Escosar, a globally respected missiologist.

To understand why it took me a while to grasp the importance of *edukasyon* in Filipino culture, it might be helpful to know that I skipped my own Mississippi State University commencement exercises and never bothered to pick up my diploma. I'm sure my diploma is now prominently displayed in the MSU Academic Hall of Fame.

My parents expected all five of their kids to graduate from university. That was non-negotiable, so all five of us graduated. However, whether we finished at the top, in the middle, or at the bottom of the class didn't really matter to them. The point was to graduate, and to have as much fun as possible along the way.

When I attempted to bring that just-as-long-as-you-graduate value to our sons, Deborah quickly raised the standard. She gathered our impressionable sons and told them, "Whatever your dad says about baseball, basketball, or anything else that involves hitting, bouncing, or throwing a ball, I want you to listen to him and do exactly what he says."

At that point I was feeling totally affirmed by my adoring wife and sons. Then she smiled at me and continued, "But when it comes to homework, grades, and school projects, I want you to only listen to me."

And that became our division of labor. I would handle sports. She would handle academics. I guess it worked out okay. All three of our sons received a combination of athletic and academic scholarships to pay for their university studies.

But back to my story about Filipino *edukasyon* and Dr. Jun Escosar's ancestral home. As soon as I stepped into the door of the Escosar family home in Iloilo, I was face-to-face with a wall covered floor-to-ceiling with scores of diplomas, academic awards, and graduation certificates for all eight kids. The Escosar *edukasyon* wall of fame included kindergarten graduation certificates, high school science fair awards, and university diplomas for every one of Jun's siblings and their parents. This was a big wall with little space left for graduate school. Not sure where they placed Jun's master's and doctorate degrees. All it takes is one step in the Escosar home, and you know they value education. And it's not just the Escosar home; it's a Filipino thing.

Just like my parents made it clear to me, Deborah and I made it clear to our sons that they would attend and graduate from university. All three excelled academically. William earned a master's degree in Medieval History from Oxford University and is now a PhD candidate in Middle Eastern History at Vanderbilt University. James overcame learning disabilities in elementary school and graduated summa cum laude from Lipscomb University's business school. Starting in high school, every semester, Jonathan created a new and improved reason he should be allowed to quit school.

> Thirteen-year-old Jonathan: "If I qualify for the US Open by the time I'm eighteen, can I skip college and just play tennis?"
>
> Me: "No."
>
> Fourteen-year-old Jonathan: "If I'm making lots of money selling my paintings, can I just skip college and be a professional artist?"
>
> Me: "No."
>
> Fifteen-year-old Jonathan: "If I start a business that is making millions before I graduate from high school, can I skip college and run my business?"
>
> Me: "No."
>
> Sixteen-year-old Jonathan: "School is a waste of my time and your money. What if you give me the money you would spend on college, and let me invest it in my business, rather than paying some boring professor to lecture me to sleep?"
>
> Me: "No."

I think you get the point. The young man didn't really embrace the importance of formal *edukasyon*, but fortunately, his parents did. And, by the grace of God and the iron will of his mother, Jonathan endured until the end, graduating with an impressive GPA (grade point average) and multiple Belmont Business School awards. Like me, Jonathan probably has no idea where his Belmont University diploma is today.

I understand that to many Filipinos, *edukasyon* is no more than collecting diplomas and degrees and pleasing parents. However, from my Western perspective, I see a people who seem to be able to learn new things and fix anything. I see a people who eventually got much more than a piece of paper with a degree. Along the educational journey, they learned to learn. Maybe it's just a Victory thing, but most of the Filipinos I work with are lifelong learners. They have the attitude of a learner, rather than the attitude of a know-it-all. I think *edukasyon* explains why the Filipinos I work with in ministry are so teachable. No matter how successful they are, they're still in learning mode. They never feel as though they've arrived. They always want to know more, learn more, be taught more, and be mentored.

Our goal in parenting was not just that our sons would earn a degree, but that they would develop a lifelong love of learning.

5. *Bayanihan* (community spirit)
It's well-documented that many Asians — not just Filipinos — are hardwired to find their place in society, to fit in, and to not rock the boat. From my limited experience, it seems the same in many African societies. Westerners, on the other hand, are usually not interested in finding their place or fitting in. They would rather stand out, break the

mold, and rock the boat. They strive to be known as rugged individuals, not great teammates.

In the West, we honor people who "pull themselves up by their bootstraps." Many boots have a loop or a bootstrap on the back of the boot that's used to pull the boot up. Figuratively, a person who pulls himself up by his bootstrap is a person who succeeded without any outside help.

Bayanihan is the opposite of bootstrapping. It's a Filipino word taken from the root word *bayan*, which refers to a country, city, or community. In other words, a group of people — not an individual. The origin of *bayanihan* goes back to a tradition of rural communities when the whole town would come together to help a family relocate their house. I've seen countless paintings of Filipino villagers carrying a straw hut on bamboo poles, helping a family literally move their house. Once the *nipa* hut has been moved to its new location, the host family throws a fiesta and feeds the town. Obviously, the family couldn't possibly have moved their home without the help of their neighbors. That's *bayanihan*.

The *bayanihan* spirit is not unique to the Philippines. In fact, it's quite common around the world. In Native American Cherokee culture it's called *gadugi*. In Sudan, they borrow an Arabic word, *naffir*. In Indonesia and Malaysia, community cooperation towards a common goal is *gotong royong*. In the Andes Mountains, it's called *mink'a*.

American individuality and Filipino *bayanihan* are opposite, but vital character traits that we attempted to cultivate in our sons. We did our best to help them understand and embrace their unique individual gifts, strengths, and calling. We wanted them to be able to "bootstrap" and go at it alone when necessary. But we also attempted to teach them to use their gifts, strengths, and calling in the context of community and for the good of others — especially those who have no bootstraps, no boots, no shoes, no opportunity, and no hope.

I'm certain that living in the Philippines for over two decades not only gave my family and me lifelong friends, but it also taught us how to do life in community better than if we had lived our whole lives in the West.

> We attempted to teach our sons to use their gifts, strengths, and calling in the context of community and for the good of others.

When my sons were ten, eight, and six, an American friend commented, "You're really lucky that your sons get along with each other. My kids are always fighting and bickering." I smiled and thanked her, but knew that luck had nothing to do with my sons getting along. Deborah and I decided they would be best friends for life, and we never tolerated anything less. We taught them (sometimes forced them) to help each other in school, on the tennis court, and with music practice. They learned to love and enjoy being with one another because we prayed they would be lifelong best friends, and we trained them to act, live, and think not strictly as individuals, but as a team, a family, and a community.

RAISING KINGDOM-CULTURE KIDS

Whether you're raising your kids in Asia, Africa, or North America, it might be a good idea to attempt instilling all five of these values deep in their souls. You can probably think of a local counterpart to the Filipino cultural values I've tried to describe. I also suggest incorporating into your kids all of the godly cultural values that are unique to your own people or tribe.

> The worst idea of all is to assume that controlling external behavior is real parenting.

Cookie-cutter, one-size-fits-all, how-to-do-it-God's-way parenting books abound, and most of us have tried and failed at various forms of behavior-modification parenting. Because we're bigger, stronger, and have the money, it's easy to make and enforce long lists of rules for our kids. Some of the items on those lists are good ideas. Some are bad ideas. The worst idea of all is to assume that controlling external behavior is real parenting.

The goal of this book is not to give you another list of dos and don'ts. You can find more than enough of those. Rather, I'm trying to encourage you to take the more difficult and time-consuming parenting journey, based on invisible character development and elusive value impartation.

The more important things in life are usually invisible and elusive. The invisible is what makes our kids who they are, for better or for worse. Entitlement, greed, bitterness, fear, and pride are all invisible yet powerfully destructive realities. On the other hand, gratefulness, generosity, loyalty, hope, and humility are invisible and internal character traits that honor God, serve people, and foster success.

As we raise Kingdom-culture kids, imparting values from our local cultures and from God's Kingdom, and as we focus on the invisible and eternal, kids and parents will experience the best of times, even during the worst of times. They will be beacons of light in seasons of darkness. They will be springs of hope in winters of despair.

DISCUSSION QUESTIONS

1. What are some local values from your own culture that you would like to instill in your children? List three to five values and brainstorm practical ways to pass these values on to your kids.

2. What are some aspects of your local/national culture that are in conflict with Kingdom values? How can you, as a parent, work to train your children to live differently?

HEART

4

THE GODFATHER
God's Heart for Children

There are many things my father taught me here in this room.
Mario Puzo, *The Godfather*

It's not personal. It's strictly business.
Mario Puzo, *The Godfather*

For you did not receive the spirit of slavery to fall back into fear, but you have received the Spirit of adoption as sons, by whom we cry, "Abba! Father!"
Romans 8:15

Every year, for as long as I can remember, one of the highlights of our Victory Manila church calendar has been our Me & My Dad Camp. Imagine a few hundred Filipino kids and their dads camping in the beautiful Sierra Madre Mountains, northeast of Manila. Great times. Great memories. Not-so-great food, cooked by culinary-challenged dads.

A Victory Me & My Dad Camp is exclusively for six- to nine-year-old kids and their dads. Campers are encouraged to bring tents, sleeping bags, food, marshmallows, bug spray, Bibles, and devotional notebooks. Campers are not allowed to bring moms, grandmothers, pets, older siblings, video consoles, satellite televisions, cooks, maids, bodyguards, or *yayas* (nannies). Air-conditioned tents are allowed.

It was always funny to see dads with daughters assembling Hello Kitty tents next to men with sons who set up campsites that look like special-ops military outposts. Thankfully, because I have three sons, I never had to camp in a pink Barbie tent. There's just something not quite right about pink gear at a campsite.

Me & My Dad Camps have always been life-changing events for the whole family. Thousands of Victory kids look back on Me & My Dad Camp as a spiritual turning point in their lives (while perhaps hundreds of Victory dads need therapy because of traumatic Me & My Dad Camp memories). Countless Victory moms became around-the-clock intercessors knowing their husbands had full responsibility to feed, clothe, and care for their helpless kids for a whole weekend.

I know some unscrupulous dads — the indoor types — who, after one Me & My Dad Camp experience, "accidentally" schedule international business trips, last-minute family vacations, or elective emergency surgery on our exact camp dates year after year.

I'm thankful for the outdoor dads (Boy Scout alumni) who made sure the indoor dads and their indoor kids made it home alive. Not sure how many kids and dads we would have lost in the Sierra Madre if not for our Victory Boy Scouts. You've done your church and humankind a great service. Your reward is surely waiting for you in heaven.

THE GODFATHER'S HEART

When my youngest son, Jonathan, was a teenager, he and I were the Me & My Dad Camp devotional speakers. I spoke to the dads in the morning and evening while Jonathan spoke to the kids. While I was teaching the dads how to discipline their kids, I have a feeling Jonathan was teaching the kids how to dodge discipline — father-son teamwork at its best.

The next year, my good friend Julius served as our devotional speaker. Julius was a good sport at these camps. He had four daughters in a row, which meant he spent a decade in a pink Barbie tent. Later, he had a boy and was finally able to spend a few years in a manly tent.

I'll never forget the year Julius was our camp devotional speaker. His Friday night topic for a couple of hundred six- to nine-year-olds and their dads was "The father heart of God." I don't know if anyone remembered the message, though I am sure it was great. What was unforgettable was the summary of his message the following morning.

> Julius to the kids: "Who remembers what we talked about last night?"
>
> Six-year-old Jeremiah raises his hand with much enthusiasm: "I know. I know. You talked about the god-father's heart!"

I wondered how many times six-year-old Jeremiah had watched *The Godfather* mob movie with his dad.

There's a big difference between the "Father heart of God" and the "Godfather's heart." In fact, they're polar opposites.

Vito Corleone, the mafia don in *The Godfather* book and movie series, had a phrase he repeated often. This phrase was foundational to his dysfunctional family and in his nefarious business dealings. Before sending his loyal mafia hit-man, Luca Brasi, to break thumbs, shoot kneecaps, or execute the competition, Vito would always explain, "It's not personal, it's just business." With mafia godfathers, it's never personal, it's always business.

Too often, many of us relate to God our Father like He's the Godfather — never personal, always business. But when we understand the Father heart of God, we realize that with Him, everything is always personal, and nothing is ever merely business. It's personal because God loves us with a father's love. He loves us so much that He gave His one and only Son as a sacrifice for our sins. It doesn't get any more personal than that.

> Too often, many of us relate to God our Father like He's the Godfather—never personal, always business.

Do you relate to God as your Father, where it's always personal, or do you relate to Him like the Godfather, where it's always business? How about your kids, do you relate to them the way God wants to relate to us, on a personal level? Or is your relationship with your kids scheduled like a business obligation?

God desires to relate to each of us and all of our children on a personal level — not like a distant stoic boss or business associate. What does it mean to relate to God as our heavenly Father?

We have all had fathers who sometimes represented and sometimes misrepresented God's heart towards us. That's why it's so important that we read and study the Bible, so we can know Him as Father.

A Surprise Valentine's Day Confession

A few years ago during our monthly Victory Manila staff meeting, Chief Operating Officer Jiji Concepcion presented us with the latest changes in our staff insurance coverage. It happened to be Valentine's Day, so before she launched into her riveting insurance speech, Jiji flashed a big smile and said she had a Valentine's Day confession for us.

As soon as Jiji mentioned that it was Valentine's Day, several married pastors discreetly pulled out their cell phones and sent emergency text messages to their assistants, who promptly pulled out their phones and placed emergency flower and chocolate delivery orders.

Jiji proceeded with her Valentine's Day confession. It centered around a story from her days as the Human Resources director at the Philippine branch of Eli Lilly, one of the largest pharmaceutical companies in the world.

When she worked at Lilly, Jiji was single, and as far as everyone in her office knew, she was not dating anyone. But every Valentine's Day, a huge bouquet of red roses would be delivered to her desk. It always had a card attached. Year after year, Jiji refused to divulge the name of her secret admirer. And every year on the big day, with the red roses dominating her desk, people would observe Jiji reading and rereading the card that accompanied the flowers. Every few hours she would read the card, smile, giggle, then return to the work on her desk. Her colleagues were relentless; they had to know the identity of her secret Valentine's Day admirer. Eventually, she caved in to the pressure and admitted that the flowers were from a man. But she told them no more. Everyone in the Lilly office speculated who the mystery man might be, but like a magician, Jiji knew how to keep a secret.

For some reason, Jiji decided that our Every Nation Philippines monthly staff meeting was the place to confess the truth that she had hidden from her Lilly friends all these years. Then she bluntly said to our whole staff that the flowers were from an older married man who said he loved her dearly. And she confessed that she also loved him.

I have never been in a staff meeting, before or since, when people paid such undivided attention to the person doing an insurance update presentation. Everyone was sitting on the edge of his or her chair, eyes glued on Jiji, as she described how loving and kind this older married man was to her. He wanted her to know that she was special—especially on Valentine's Day.

I had a good guess where this story was going. I was pretty sure I knew the married man she was talking about; the man who sent the flowers and who had loved her all these years.

Then Jiji said his name. I was right. It was the man I suspected. He was married, and he definitely loved her then and still loves her today and talks about her all the time. I know this because he's a good friend of mine. This man would do anything for her. Anything. Anytime. And the fact that Jiji is now married hasn't changed a thing. The Valentine's Day flower man would still do anything for her.

Because of the theme of this chapter, you probably guessed the identity of Jiji's married flower man. But in case you're still wondering, that older married man who sent her flowers every Valentine's Day was her dad, and my good friend, Salvador Fabregas. All his friends call him Bomboy.

Bomboy wanted his youngest unmarried adult daughter to know that her dad loved her. He wanted her to know that even if she was single, someone loved and adored her with his whole heart. So he sent flowers.

As Jiji ended her story and transitioned to the new insurance policies, some people in the room were laughing, others were discreetly wiping tears. I imagined I could hear unspoken cries in the hearts of many saying, "I wish I had a father who loved me like that." Others were thinking, "I'm sure my father loves me. I just wish he would express his love." The pastor in me wanted to grab the mic and tell them that they do have a Father who loves them and expresses His love like that. In fact, He loves every one of us more than an earthly father could ever love a son or daughter.

But the problem is that we often relate to him as the Godfather—always business, never personal. This will only change when we understand the Father heart of God towards us.

MR. GOD OR ABBA FATHER?

The idea of relating to God as a father was as foreign to Old Testament people as it is to many religious people today. The original disciples often heard Jesus referring to God as "Father" during their prayer times together. When they asked Jesus to teach them to pray, He taught them to pray to their "Father in heaven." As the Gospels move forward, page by page, year by year, I'm sure the disciples got used to hearing Jesus pray to His heavenly Father. And I'm sure some of them even got comfortable relating to God the Father in a New Covenant personal relationship, rather than to the Godfather in an Old Covenant business manner.

At the end of His life on earth, while on the cross, Jesus took the "Father in heaven" thing to a whole new level. At the most painful moment of His crucifixion, Jesus prayed, "*Abba, Father,* all things are possible for you. Remove this cup from me. Yet not what I will, but what you will" (Mark 14:36).

The phrase *Abba Father* is used only two other times in Scripture. It's a combination of a similar word in two different languages. *Abba* is a familiar, informal Aramaic word for father. In Jesus' prayer in Mark 14, *Abba* is followed by the word Father. It seems redundant, but not when we catch the nuanced meaning of the two words. Father is translated from the Greek word *pater* and is a more formal word for father than its Aramaic counterpart.

During the three years that Jesus discipled the original twelve, He helped them get comfortable calling God their Father. That was a big step from the way their Old Testament heroes talked to God. One of His final messages from the cross was for them to take their relationship with God a step further by relating to Him not only as a formal Father, but also as an informal *Abba*. The American English equivalent of *Abba* is Daddy or Papa. Father is formal. *Abba* or Daddy is informal and more personal.

Paul reinforced this idea that we can know God, not only as a formal heavenly Father, but also as a relational Daddy. Twice he used the *Abba Father* title that Jesus used on the cross.

When Paul was trying to get the disciples in Rome to understand that God desired a personal relationship, not a business relationship with them, he quoted Jesus on the cross. "For you did not receive the spirit of slavery to fall back into fear, but you have received the Spirit of adoption as sons, by whom we cry, *'Abba! Father!'"* (Romans 8:15)

To the legalistic disciples in Galatia, Paul also quotes Jesus on the cross. "And because you are sons, God has sent the Spirit of his Son into our hearts, crying, *'Abba! Father!'"* (Galatians 4:6)

Some of you have experienced the awkward transition that sometimes happens when you get engaged and married. What do I call my new in-laws? When Deborah and I got married, my parents wanted her to call them by their first names, Jim and Betsy. I'm sure that was a bit uncomfortable for Deborah for a season, but in time, it seemed perfectly natural.

In the Philippines, most people call their spouse's parents "Mom" and "Dad." My second daughter-in-law is a Fil-Am, half-Filipino and half-American. A couple of months before she and Jonathan got married, she asked if she could call me Pops. (William and James have always called me Dad.

Jonathan, our creative one, has always called me Pops.) I imagine her transition from calling me "Pastor Steve" to "Pops" might have been a bit awkward at first, but now that my granddaughter calls me "Pops", it seems like everyone is getting more and more comfortable addressing me as "Pops".

In the same way, I'm sure the disciples found it a bit unnerving to address God as their Father, rather than as a distant deity whose name was too holy to pronounce. It had to be an even greater shock to their religious mindset to now be told to address Him as *Abba*, but I'm sure that, in time, they got used to it as they grew closer to Him.

THE MOST POPULAR STORY IN THE BIBLE

No matter what kind of father you had on earth, you have a Father in heaven who loves you fully. The most read, studied, and preached story in the Bible paints a picture of God as a loving, forgiving father to rebellious and self-righteous children who seem to always want to run from Him.

Before we get to that famous father story, we need to understand why Jesus told the story in the first place.

Luke 15 records that Jesus, as usual, was hanging out with some unsavory characters. The Bible called them "tax collectors and sinners." In biblical times, tax collectors were usually Jewish people who had turned their backs on their religion and on their people by collaborating with the hated Roman occupiers. They knew better, but for the sake of money or because of peer pressure, they compromised and oppressed their own people.

The people referred to as "sinners" in this story are not Jewish compromisers, but people who had no training in Scripture and no knowledge of the one true God. They were immoral idolaters who didn't know any better. They were also known as heathens, pagans, and Greeks.

In the pages of Scripture, Jesus seemed to always be hanging around sinners and tax collectors. Today we don't call them sinners and tax collectors; we call them backsliders and non-religious. Missiologists call them de-churched and un-churched.

As always, the overly pious religious leaders — known as Pharisees and scribes — criticized Jesus for reaching out to these de-churched and un-churched people whom they deemed to be far from God.

Jesus told three stories in Luke 15 to explain why he always spent so much time with sinners and tax collectors, de-churched and un-churched people, and backsliders and non-religious people.

One Lost Sheep

The first story was about a shepherd who had a hundred sheep. Today we don't know anything about shepherds and sheep, but everyone listening to Jesus was as familiar with shepherds and sheep as we are with lattes and cappuccinos. Jesus explained what they already knew — that a good shepherd would leave his ninety-nine sheep to look for the one that was lost. After finding his one lost sheep, Jesus says, the shepherd called all his friends and threw a homecoming party for the sheep. Jesus ended the story saying, "Just so, I tell you, there will be more joy in heaven over one sinner who repents than over ninety-nine righteous persons who need no repentance."

One Lost Coin

The second story Jesus told was about a woman who lost a coin. Jesus explained that she looked and looked until she found it. Then, when she finally found the coin, she called all her friends and, like the shepherds, had an I-found-my-lost-coin party—probably spending more on the party than the coin was worth in the first place. Jesus ended the second story by saying, "Just so, I tell you, there is joy before the angels of God over one sinner who repents."

Two Lost Sons

The third story is much longer and more famous than the first two. Today we call this story the Parable of the Prodigal Son. Whoever named it must not have read the whole story, because there were two prodigals, not one. Plus the Prodigal Son title misses the point that the central character is the compassionate father, not the rebellious son or the self-righteous son.

> What a father does with his hands says volumes about him.

Here's my summary of the story. A father has two sons. The younger son can't wait for his father to die, so he demands an inheritance early (while his father is still alive). As soon as he gets the money, he leaves for a distant land where he dishonors his father's name, breaks his father's heart, and squanders his father's hard-earned money on wild parties and loose women.

Sooner than later, he runs out of money. When he was with his father, he had more than enough. The farther he gets from his father and the longer he's away from his father, the less he has, until he finally has nothing. That's the way it always works when we dishonor fathers.

Eventually, the rebellious young son comes to his senses and returns home, hoping his father will hire him as a farmhand or a household servant.

Jesus narrates, "But while he was still a long way off, his father saw him and felt compassion, and ran and embraced him and kissed him" (Luke 15:20).

What a beautiful picture of our heavenly Father. No matter how far we run from Him, no matter how much we dishonor His name with wild living, as soon as we turn towards Him, even if we're still far off, He has compassion for us. He runs to us.

Now watch His hands. Jesus says this father "embraced" or hugged his wayward son. What a father does with his hands says volumes about him.

The Hands of God

Many of us rebelled and dishonored our fathers. When we returned, some of us were met with hands that embraced us with a compassionate hug—just like the prodigal in the Bible. But others of us were met with hands that were less than compassionate.

- **The finger of guilt.** Maybe when you returned home from your season of rebellion, you were met by a hand pointing an index finger of accusation. A long finger pointing out everything you did wrong. A judgmental finger saying, "I told you so." The pointing finger of fatherly accusation produces guilt deep in the heart of sons and daughters who are trying to find their way back home.

- **The slap of shame.** For others it was not the index finger of guilt, but the open palm of shame. As you returned home, maybe you were met with hands that brought a humiliating slap to the face, accompanied with familiar words of shame. The disappointed father who slaps a son or daughter creates a deep sense of shame in the heart of his kids.

- **The fist of rejection.** For others, it went beyond pointing fingers and open-handed slaps. Some of you were met with a hand that was balled into a fist that struck your face, accompanied with familiar words of anger and rage. Violent hands—especially those attached to fathers—send a soul-shattering message of rejection that tends to grow in the heart of kids long after they're no longer kids. Unfortunately, violence begets violence, generation after generation.

> This is what fathers do. They go after their kids—no matter what those kids do. They welcome them home.

- **The embrace of forgiveness.** The judgmental finger that points out mistakes, the open hand that slaps, and the clenched fist that hits are not the hands of the prodigal's father in the story, and they're not the hands of our heavenly Father. They shouldn't be our hands either. Our heavenly Father is reaching out to us in compassionate love, to embrace us and welcome us back into His family, no matter how far we have strayed. When we understand the hand God extended to us, we can then extend His hand to our own children. When we've experienced the compassionate embrace of the Father, we can give that hug of acceptance to our own kids.

The heart of parenting is to accept, know, and understand God as Father. Then we will begin to see our children the way God sees us, and we will begin to treat them the way our heavenly Father treats us.

Psalm 103:13 says that, "As a father shows compassion to his children, so the Lord shows compassion to those who fear him." Here, the psalmist assumes that fathers treat their kids with loving compassion. Therefore, he presents all fathers as a picture of how our heavenly Father treats us. But because we have so many dysfunctional fathers today, we need to use our loving heavenly Father as a picture of how a real father is supposed to relate to kids.

After embracing his wayward son with hands of compassion, the prodigal's father tells his servants to "Bring quickly the best robe, and put it on him, and put a ring on his hand, and shoes on his feet. And bring the fattened calf and kill it, and let us eat and celebrate. For this my son was dead, and is alive again; he was lost, and is found" (Luke 15:22-24). Like the shepherd who found his lost sheep and the woman who found her lost coin, the father gives his best and throws a welcome home party when he finds his lost son. Notice, he didn't give an "I-told-you-so" or a "this-is-your-last-chance" speech. He gave a party!

The Other Lost Son

The older son, who had patiently waited for his inheritance and dutifully served his father, was less than happy to have his prodigal brother back in the house. Here's how Jesus described the scene. "But he was angry and refused to go in. His father came out and entreated him" (Luke 15:28).

The young son was rebellious. The older son was self-righteous. Both turned away from their father. The father ran to the rebellious young son and welcomed him home. The father went after the self-righteous older son and pleaded for him to come home.

This is what fathers do. They go after their kids — no matter what those kids do. They welcome them home. They embrace them with loving compassion. This is the heart of parenting. This is also the heart of God towards each of us.

Turning the Hearts of the Fathers

The last verse in the Old Testament gives me great hope for all parents and their kids — especially those kids who have wandered far from home. The prophet Malachi says that a time is coming when "he will turn the hearts of fathers to their children and the hearts of children to their fathers" (Malachi 4:6). I pray that as you read this book, God will work on your heart. I pray He will turn it towards your kids. It doesn't matter how old they are, I'm trusting God that your heart will turn. It doesn't matter how long it's been since you felt close to them, I'm praying God will turn hearts.

And I'm praying that as God turns your heart towards your kids, He will simultaneously start turning their hearts towards you.

It all starts with the heart. When God changes the heart, it's only a matter of time until attitudes and actions change. That's what the heart of parenting is all about.

DISCUSSION QUESTIONS

1. Which of the four types of "hands" best characterizes your relationship with your parents (finger of guilt, slap of shame, fist of rejection, embrace of forgiveness)? How has that affected (for better or for worse) how you parent?

2. When/how did you receive a revelation of God as your Father?

3. How does a revelation of God as our heavenly Father affect how you parent?

5

THE HEART OF DARKNESS
Every Child's Heart

*I felt an intolerable weight oppressing my breast . . .
the unseen presence of victorious corruption,
the darkness of an impenetrable night.*
Joseph Conrad, *The Heart of Darkness*

*It echoed loudly within him because he was
hollow at the core.*
Joseph Conrad, *The Heart of Darkness*

*Folly is bound up in the heart of a child, but the rod
of discipline drives it far from him.*
Proverbs 22:15

Joseph Conrad's novel, *The Heart of Darkness*, explores the universality of the heart of darkness, no matter how sophisticated the outward surroundings may look. The narrator, Charles Marlow, is sitting on a boat anchored in England on the Thames River, telling the story of an ivory trader on the Congo River in the heart of Africa. As the story unfolds, it seems that Conrad is exposing the darkness in "civilized" London by contrasting it with the darkness in "uncivilized" Africa.

There comes a time in every parent's life when they realize that their perfect baby isn't perfect. In a moment, they realize that their child — who could do no wrong — is actually quite good at it. Some parents accept the universality of the heart of darkness while others pretend that their little angel is the only exception to Original Sin.

With my oldest son, William, the realization came quickly — as he was an early crawler, walker, and talker. But if we had any reason to chalk up his apparent rebellion to simply being a strong-willed child, all it took was one disastrous Christmas Eve at my in-laws' to convince us that our adorable three-year-old was far from perfect, and that the doctrine of Original Sin is still true.

OUR CHRISTMAS EVE DISASTER

The year was 1989. William was three and a half. James, our second son, was eighteen months. Our youngest, Jonathan, wouldn't be born for two more months.

This was the year William realized that Christmas meant gifts. At an early stage, we had attempted to teach our boys the true meaning of Christmas. We told them the Christmas story from the Bible. We explained the Advent wreath. We watched *It's a Wonderful Life*. We didn't expect much from our eighteen-month-old, but we assumed that William had caught the Christmas spirit — giving (not getting). You know, "God so loved the world that He gave His only Son . . ."

However, what happened that night let us know that William had completely missed the point, and we had already failed as parents.

All William wanted for Christmas that year was a bow and arrow. His little mind was made up. He knew what he wanted and he would not be denied. He prayed to God for it, and just to be sure, he begged us for it.

One day, to make sure I understood his request, he said, "Daddy, I want real arrows."

"Real arrows?" I asked, wondering what kind of damage a three-year-old could do with real arrows.

"Yeah, you know the kind with the red rubber things on the end. Real ones, not just toys." He was serious about this.

"You mean the kind that stick to windows if you lick 'em before shooting?" I responded, hoping I knew what he meant.

"Yeah! Like in Toys-R-Us."

At our Christmas Eve gathering at my in-laws', James was first to open his gifts. Like all eighteen-month-olds, he was more impressed with the colorful boxes and ribbons than with the contents.

Then came William's turn. As James continued to play with bows and boxes, William anxiously ripped through his first gift in world record time. He completely ignored the contents and immediately tore into the next one. He only got the wrapping paper halfway off this one before tossing it aside and grabbing the next one. And so began the epic Christmas Eve meltdown.

Deborah and I discerned that something was going terribly wrong, but what could we do?

Surrounded by half-opened gifts, William slumped over and began to cry. "I thought I would get a bow and arrow, with real arrows." He mumbled through the tears. "That's all I wanted, and I didn't get it. I got all this other stuff instead."

What he didn't realize was that underneath the pile of shredded wrapping paper and half-opened gifts was a bow with "real" (rubber-tipped) arrows. But he was too busy throwing a tantrum and humiliating his young parents.

It seemed as though our precious little three-year-old, in his cute Christmas sweater, had transformed before our eyes into the picture of ingratitude and human selfishness.

How could this have happened? We were raising him in a loving home. We took him to church every Sunday. We provided for all of his needs and most of his wants (including a bow and arrow). How could he be so selfish?

Basically Good or Totally Depraved?

Ask most child development "experts" today, and they'll tell you that my three-year-old was a *good* child who just happened to exhibit *bad* behavior at an inopportune time. William's apparent selfishness and ingratitude weren't a reflection of who he was deep down inside, but rather unfortunate consequences of a misunderstanding or an unfulfilled need.

The essential goodness of human nature — especially in children — is the basic framework through which most parents in the West interpret their children's behavior. Good behavior is natural; bad behavior is an exception — the consequence of external influences, socioeconomics, psychological needs, or blood-moon cycles. As a result, good parenting is about dealing with bad behavior and understanding each child's individual needs.

The idea that children are basically good but occasionally exhibit bad behavior is an attractive one that's espoused in talk shows, parenting books, educational institutions, and popular media.

But the one place you won't find this idea is in the Bible.

If twenty-first century parenting wisdom assumes the essential goodness of humanity, ancient biblical parenting wisdom assumes the exact opposite.

According to the Bible, the problem with my three-year-old was not behavioral, socioeconomic, or even psychological. The problem had to do with his heart. For deep down inside, beneath the charming smile and the chubby cheeks and the cute Christmas sweater, William was not basically good. He was sinful.

According to the Bible, children are not essentially good, and bad behavior is not an exception. Rather, children, like their parents, are essentially sinful, and bad behavior is natural.

Here are just a few examples of what the Bible says about the human heart, including the child's heart:

- ". . . for the intention of man's heart is evil from his youth. . . ." (Genesis 8:21).

- "Behold, I was brought forth in iniquity, and in sin did my mother conceive me" (Psalm 51:5).

- "Folly is bound up in the heart of a child, but the rod of discipline drives it far from him" (Proverbs 22:15).

- "The heart is deceitful above all things, and desperately sick; who can understand it?" (Jeremiah 17:9)

- "For I know that nothing good dwells in me, that is, in my flesh . . . For I do not do the good I want, but the evil I do not want is what I keep on doing" (Romans 7:18–19).

While these verses may seem harsh at first glance, think about your own experience and see if Paul's words in Romans don't mirror the condition of your own heart: "I do not do the good I want, but the evil I do not want is what I keep on doing."

These verses outline the ancient biblical doctrine of Original Sin. The idea that as a result of the Fall (see Genesis 3), at the core of their being, people are sinful and their hearts are inclined to selfishness, ingratitude, and evil—whether they're a three-year-old in a Christmas sweater or a convicted felon in an orange jumpsuit.

Far from seeing children as basically good, Saint Augustine succinctly described the parenting implications of the doctrine of Original Sin for the fourth century family: "The only innocent feature in babies is the weakness of their frames; the minds of infants are far from innocent." That statement was true 1,600 years ago, and it's still true today.

WILDFLOWERS AND "NATURAL" PARENTING

If what the Bible says about human nature is true, then it has profound implications on parenting. Most importantly, parenting is not primarily about dealing with bad behavior; it's about dealing with bad hearts.

So how do we deal with the surprisingly sinful heart of a child?

Two words: discipline and training.

If these words come across to you as stern, heartless, and needlessly old-fashioned, it's because we live in a society that idolizes individual freedom and believes in the fundamental goodness of humanity (as opposed to Original Sin).

In other words, if children are basically good, needing only occasional behavioral corrections, they should *naturally* grow up into morally upright and responsible adults. Discipline and training, therefore, are unnecessary and will only serve to stunt natural growth and individuality.

According to this wisdom, children are like wildflowers. Give them space and sunlight, and nature will do the rest.

However, if we believe what the Bible says about the human heart, then we understand that our children are less like wildflowers and more like garden flowers. They need more than just space and sunlight. They need to be watered, tended, and weeded. Like plants in a garden, we can't just leave our children to grow up naturally. If we do, they'll turn out like a neglected garden flower — dried up, overcome with weeds, and exhibiting all the wrong kinds of growth.

Though "natural" parenting is becoming a twenty-first century phenomenon, it's not new. Over 250 years ago, Jean-Jacques Rousseau articulated the natural approach to parenting in his influential book on education, *Emile*. In this book, the famous Genevan philosopher argued that discipline and training from parents and educators disrupted the natural development of children. He argued that what children really needed was freedom from parental and institutional interference.

Because of his belief in the fundamental goodness of children, Rousseau encouraged parents to "hold childhood in reverence, and do not be in any hurry to judge it for good or ill." And instead to "give nature time to work before you take over her business, lest you interfere with her dealings."

THE IMPORTANCE OF RESTRAINING REBELLION

One parent in the Bible tried "natural" parenting nearly 3,000 years before Rousseau wrote about it — Eli, the high priest of Israel. He, along with his sons, Hophni and Phinehas, served at the Tabernacle in Shiloh — before the Temple was built in Jerusalem. We don't know how old his sons were (probably young men), but the first thing we find out about them in the Bible is this: "Now the sons of Eli were worthless men. They did not know the Lord" (1 Samuel 2:12).

As priests, Hophni and Phinehas were responsible for helping Israelites offer sacrifices at the Tabernacle. Instead, they
would often steal the meat of the goat or sheep during the
sacrifice before the fire had burned it up. The Bible says,
"Thus the sin of the young men was very great in the sight
of the Lord, for the men treated the offering of the Lord with
contempt" (1 Samuel 2:17).

Not only were Hophni and Phinehas stealing from the people,
but they were sleeping with the women who volunteered to
serve at the Tabernacle.

What's sad about this story is that Eli didn't seem to realize
what was happening right beneath his nose! He seems to
have been the kind of parent who left his sons lots of space
and sunlight to let them grow up "naturally." He gave them
so much space that someone else had to tell him about what
Hophni and Phinehas were doing. "Now Eli was very old,
and he kept hearing all that his sons were doing to all Israel,
and how they lay with the women who were serving at the
entrance to the tent of meeting" (1 Samuel 2:22).

After learning about his sons' wickedness, Eli tried to
plead with his sons, but it was too little too late. "And he
said to them, 'Why do you do such things? For I hear of
your evil dealings from all these people. No, my sons; it is
no good report that I hear the people of the Lord spreading
abroad. . . .' But they would not listen to the voice of their
father" (1 Samuel 2:23-25).

Making Excuses or Admitting Guilt?

Eli made the classic mistake that parents still make today. He asked his sons *why* they disobeyed. When parents ask why, they train their children to justify disobedience and make excuses. Rather than asking questions that lead to excuses and justification, wise parents ask questions that reveal truth and establish guilt. The wisest parent ever, God, did not ask Adam and Eve *why* they ate the mango. He asked a yes or no question with no room for an excuse. *"Have you* eaten of the tree of which I commanded you not to eat?"* (Genesis 3:11). While this question demands a simple yes or no answer, Adam still attempted an excuse — blaming it on the woman.

> Rather than asking questions that lead to excuses and justification, wise parents ask questions that reveal truth and establish guilt.

Don't make the mistake Eli made by asking questions that prompt excuses. Rather, follow the example of the best Father ever and ask questions that demand truth and establish guilt. Forgiveness happens only after guilt has been established and admitted.

As the High Priest and (more importantly) as their father, Eli should have stopped Hophni and Phinehas's wickedness in the Tabernacle long before it got to the point that it did. But because Eli failed to actively discipline and train his sons, they not only oppressed the people they were meant to serve, they brought the judgment of God on Eli's family line — which was cut off from priestly service forever.

In a pronouncement of judgment, God said, "On that day I will fulfill against Eli all that I have spoken concerning his house, from beginning to end. And I declare to him that I am about to punish his house forever, for the iniquity that he knew, because his sons were blaspheming God, and he did not restrain them" (1 Samuel 3:12-13).

Those last few words of this tragic story explain a lot.

God wasn't judging Eli because his sons rebelled. God was judging Eli because "he did not restrain them." He knew they were sinning, and he didn't actively intrude upon their freedom and apply discipline and training to their lives. Hophni and Phinehas are a classic example of garden flowers left to grow naturally. They were spiritually dead. They were covered in weeds. And they exhibited fruitless and ultimately destructive growth.

Just to repeat — this story shouldn't be seen as a cautionary tale to all parents of wayward children. Children rebel for a variety of reasons. Sometimes the parents are at fault, and sometimes they aren't. What we should learn from this story is that while parents are not completely responsible for their children's behavior, they are responsible to water and tend to their children — this includes actively weeding out rebellious attitudes and destructive habits.

TEACHING KIDS TO DISCERN GOD'S VOICE

So if "natural" parenting is the wrong way to go, what does it look like to actively and intentionally discipline and train our children?

Without getting too caught up in technical definitions, I would say that discipline and training are like two sides of a coin. Discipline has to do with restraining destructive attitudes and behaviors—what Eli failed to do with Hophni and Phinehas. And training has to do with teaching and imparting godly attitudes and habits—what Eli learned to do with Samuel.

The story of Samuel can be seen as a moment of redemption in Eli's life. He failed as a father, but in his old age, God gave him the opportunity to be a surrogate father to Samuel.

Samuel's training under Eli began early, for Samuel was dedicated by his mother at birth to serve God in the Tabernacle. This meant that Samuel spent most of his waking hours at the aged Eli's side. Samuel would have learned about the sacrificial system instituted by Moses and heard the stories of the Exodus and the Red Sea crossing and the conquest of Canaan.

However, Samuel's defining childhood moment would come one night in the Tabernacle when he heard a voice calling his name.

In 1 Samuel 3:4–5, we read, "Then the Lord called Samuel, and he said, 'Here I am!' and ran to Eli and said, 'Here I am, for you called me.' But he said, 'I did not call; lie down again.' So he went and lay down."

Again God called Samuel. And again, he woke up old Eli, who immediately (and probably grumpily) sent him back to bed.

It happened a third time, but this time, "Eli perceived that the Lord was calling the boy. Therefore Eli said to Samuel, 'Go, lie down, and if he calls you, you shall say, "Speak, Lord, for your servant hears"'" (1 Samuel 3:8–9).

So Samuel went back to bed. And God called him a fourth time. "And Samuel said, 'Speak, for your servant hears.'" (1 Samuel 3:10).

This life-changing moment — made possible by Eli's involvement in Samuel's life — was the beginning of two important things for Samuel. First, this was the foundation of Samuel's career as a prophet. That night was the first time God had spoken to Samuel and it wouldn't be the last.

But second, and more importantly, that night was the start of Samuel's relationship with God. In 1 Samuel 3:7, when Samuel was confused about who was calling him, we read, "Now Samuel did not yet know the Lord, and the word of the Lord had not yet been revealed to him." This little note by the author is a helpful reminder that even children who have literally grown up in church, as Samuel did, still need to have their own encounter with God — a moment or series of moments when God becomes real to them.

What's important to point out here is that God used Eli in this process. Who knows what would have happened had Eli not taught Samuel how to recognize and respond to God's voice? When Eli told Samuel to say, "Speak, Lord, for your servant hears," he wasn't functioning as a priest but as a father.

Think about it. The boy he had been raising in the Tabernacle was waking him up at night and saying that he was hearing things. Old Eli could have easily sent him back to bed—as he did twice. Instead, he realized that God was working in Samuel's life. But Samuel needed someone to teach him how to recognize and respond to God's voice. The Bible doesn't say it, but this was probably just the first of many occasions where the young prophet sought help from his spiritual father, Eli.

DISCIPLINE, TRAINING, AND HELICOPTER PARENTS

Every child is born with a sinful nature, and every parent will have to confront the fact that (no matter how cute and photogenic) his or her child is sinful at heart.

If the story of Eli's sons, Hophni and Phinehas, gives us a picture of "natural" parenting and its conse-quences, then the story of Samuel gives us a picture of biblical parenting and its potential.

The key difference between Samuel and his rebellious older "brothers" was not Samuel's superior goodness. The difference was Eli's active involvement in disciplin-ing and training Samuel—something he failed to do with Hophni and Phinehas.

I don't know how many times people have told Deborah and me how lucky we are that we have such well-behaved, respectful sons. Implicit in their compliment is the assump-tion that we just happened to get three "good ones." In other words, how our children turned out had little to do with our roles as parents and more to do with the luck of the draw.

As one of my relatives used to say, "You shouldn't have more than two or three kids, because the more you have, the greater the chance that you'll get a *bad one*."

According to the Bible, we always get bad ones.

I'm not saying that children aren't intrinsically valuable and worthy of love (they are); I'm saying that children aren't inherently good. Every child is born with a sinful nature, and every parent will have to confront the fact that (no matter how cute and photogenic) his or her child is sinful at heart.

As a result, the job of parents is not to let their children grow up "naturally" or pray that they'll be lucky enough to get good ones; our job is to discipline and train our children. As Solomon said in Proverbs 22:6, "Train up a child in the way he should go; even when he is old he will not depart from it."

But here's the question: How do we as parents know "the way" that our children should go? How closely should we monitor their attitudes and behavior? How active should we be in their lives—and for how long?

In other words, what distinguishes biblical parenting from helicopter parenting?

If you're not familiar with the term, according to *Wikipedia*, "a helicopter parent" is one "who pays extremely close attention to a child's or children's experiences and problems, particularly at educational institutions. Helicopter parents are so named because, like helicopters, they hover overhead."

They obsess about their children's diet, worrying about what bad food their children might ingest at a sleepover. They pester their children's teachers at school, worrying that one bad test score in the second grade will ruin their chances of getting accepted at Harvard or Cambridge. Some even make their child wear a helmet, elbow pads, kneepads, and shin guards when playing Wii Fit.

In other words, helicopter parents hover. I bring this up because it seems that many well-meaning Christians today often confuse biblical parenting with helicopter parenting.

What's the difference?

Sometimes it can be hard to tell because both kinds of parents may do very similar things in certain cases. However, what really distinguishes between the two kinds of parenting is how they define "the way."

Both types of parents may closely monitor their children's media consumption. Both types of parents may encourage their children to work hard in school. Both types of parents may instill a respect for authority. And both types of parents may exercise similar disciplinary practices.

But the real question is why? What are we trying to accomplish by doing these things as parents?

Why are you monitoring what movies your children watch? Why are you instilling work ethic in your children? Why are you teaching them good manners and respect for authority? Why are you correcting and restraining bad behavior?

WHICH WAY IS THE RIGHT WAY?

Helicopter parents may have a variety of reasons for their parenting style—some very practical and some rather arbitrary. But with biblical parenting, we have only one ultimate motive—to point our children to God. In the book of Deuteronomy, Moses summed up "the way" to the people of Israel:

> Love the Lord your God with all your heart and with all your soul and with all your strength. These commandments that I give you today are to be on your hearts. Impress them on your children. Talk about them when you sit at home and when you walk along the road, when you lie down and when you get up. (Deuteronomy 6: 5–7, NIV)

So what is "the way" we want to raise our children? What's the point of taking an active role in disciplining and training our children?

It's about teaching them *who* to love — God.

It's about teaching them *how* to love — with all of their hearts.

It's about teaching them *what* to obey — the Word of God.

It's about teaching them *how* to obey it — by impressing it on their hearts.

This way isn't something that can simply be learned in a Sunday school class. This way isn't something that your teenagers can pick up by merely going to youth group every Friday. This way is something that's primarily transferred from parent to child at home and in all of life.

Whether we're carefully monitoring their media consumption, encouraging them to work hard in school, or instilling in them a respect for authority or correcting a bad attitude—every act of parenting should be about shaping our child's heart, not about controlling behavior.

Every act of parenting is about preparing them to encounter Jesus. The one who claimed "I am the way, and the truth, and the life. No one comes to the Father except through me" (John 14:6).

FATHER, SON, AND THE HOLY SPIRIT

I had just said the last "Amen," dismissing the second morning worship service. People were still crowding the altar. Some requested prayer for healing, some for salvation. Others just needed a little encouragement. As usual, I was directing traffic, referring this person to the youth pastor, that person to a small group leader.

Finally, when it looked like everyone's needs were covered, my wife tapped me on the shoulder: "Steve, he wants you to pray for him."

He wanted me to pray for him. He wouldn't settle for one of the other pastors or staff. It had to be me.

While I'd known him for six years, I'd never seen him so serious. I motioned for him to sit down with me on the steps right in front of the pulpit. I put my arm around his shoulder and asked, "So, what do you want me to pray for?"

After nervously studying his feet for a few minutes, he said: ". . . Um, I just want to be closer to Jesus."

This guy was serious. He really wanted to know God. A year ago, I had invited him to attend a showing of the *Jesus* film at our student center in Manila's University Belt. That night, he received Jesus as his Lord and Savior, but this was different. God was doing a deeper work in his heart, and he was responding.

Of all the people in the congregation, he was the last one I expected to request prayer that morning. Actually, I was a little surprised to find out he even listened to my sermon. He never took notes or even looked up the Scriptures I referenced. Nevertheless, the Holy Spirit had gotten through to him. I led him in a prayer of dedication and consecration.

> Parenting is all about helping kids get closer to Jesus.

After we both said "Amen," he looked up at me. His serious look had been replaced with a shy grin. His eyes glowed with a peace that only comes from knowing the Lord. God answered our prayer that day. He's closer to Jesus now than ever before. That's what church is all about — helping people get closer to Jesus.

And that's also what parenting is all about — helping kids get closer to Jesus.

So why did this guy insist that I pray for him? Why not one of the other pastors? It wasn't because I was the senior pastor. It had nothing to do with my title or position in the church. It wouldn't have made any difference to him if I were the senior pastor or the lobby janitor. So why did it have to be me?

Because I'm his dad.

In the same way Samuel needed Eli to help him recognize and respond to the Holy Spirit, my son William — of Christmas Eve infamy — needed me to help him respond to the Holy Spirit that Sunday morning.

In the next chapter, we'll take a deeper look at our role as parents, but one important aspect from both stories that can be easily overlooked is the role of the Holy Spirit. We can do everything right as parents, but if the Holy Spirit doesn't transform the sinful heart of our children, then our labor as parents will be in vain. Samuel may have needed Eli to teach him how to recognize God's voice, but it was the Holy Spirit who was calling him that night. William may have needed his dad to pray with him to be closer to God, but it was the Holy Spirit who was drawing him that Sunday morning.

If you find the reality of Original Sin a daunting obstacle to your success as a parent, then I have good news for you. As parents, we're in a partnership with the Holy Spirit and He ultimately is the one who softens and transforms the deeply sinful human heart — whether it's the heart of a strong-willed three-year-old, a rebellious teenager, or a wayward adult.

DISCUSSION QUESTIONS

1. What approach best characterizes the way your parents raised you? Were they "natural" parents, letting you do whatever you wanted? Were they "helicopter" parents who micromanaged your life? Or did they adopt a healthy biblical balance of parental involvement, discipline, and trust?

2. What kinds of challenges have you encountered disciplining and training your children at different ages?

3. How have you learned to partner with the Holy Spirit as you raise your children?

6

WAR AND PEACE
Every Parent's Heart

> *To understand all is to forgive all.*
>
> Leo Tolstoy, *War and Peace*
>
> *The strongest of all warriors are these two — Time and Patience.*
>
> Leo Tolstoy, *War and Peace*
>
> *For though we walk in the flesh, we are not waging war according to the flesh.*
>
> 2 Corinthians 10:3

Having established that the heart of every child — because of sin — is a heart of darkness until the light of the gospel enters and transforms it, we will now look at the heart of the parent. Like every child's heart, the heart of every parent is broken because of Original Sin. And like the heart of a child, the heart of a parent can be transformed by the gospel of Christ.

The prophet Ezekiel predicted a day when the gospel would transform our evil hearts and give us new hearts. "And I will give you a new heart, and a new spirit I will put within you. And I will remove the heart of stone from your flesh and give you a heart of flesh" (Ezekiel 36:26).

The gospel gives us hope as parents — hope that God can transform our children and hope that He is still working on us.

In the meantime, between complete transformation and fallen reality, parenting often seems like an endless cycle of war and peace — hopefully followed by more peace and less war. Many of the wars are fought inside the parents' minds and hearts. Most of the victories are won when the parents are on their knees.

I'm not sure, but maybe Tolstoy's never-ending novel, *War and Peace*, was actually a parable about parents and their kids rather than a novel about a Napoleonic war with Russia.

Assuming Tolstoy wasn't writing about parenting, I think he'll forgive me for applying his wise words to our topic at hand. "The strongest of all warriors are these two — Time and Patience." Whether you're in a time of parental war or a time of parental peace, time and patience are your friends.

LEGOS, PARENTING, AND OPTIONAL INSTRUCTION MANUALS

When my sons were in elementary school, they loved building stuff out of Lego. So did I. Some of our most epic time and patience lessons happened on the Lego battlefields.

For years, no birthday was complete without a new Lego set. And nearly every Christmas, Deborah and I would get the boys one of those giant Lego forts or aircraft that came with War-and-Peace-sized instruction manuals. Actually, building what was pictured on the box required an architectural degree, an engineering team, and six months.

When my sons were younger, I did most of the instruction-reading and Lego construction on Christmas day. My sons were in charge of demolition. However, as they got older, our Christmas day Lego tradition became more of a team effort. When our oldest son, William, could read, I gladly handed over the baton as instruction-reader and joined James in following William's orders on where to put what and what to build next.

The only member of our team who resisted William's capable leadership was Jonathan, our youngest.

Usually in a world of his own, Jonathan preferred to construct his Legos with little or no reference to the instructions. The rest of us may have been building Lego's Ice Planet while Jonathan was using our silver and blue pieces to build a zoo for his toy animals or a parking garage for his Hot Wheels. It wasn't that he was incapable of following the directions. He just preferred to do it his way. Ironically, Jonathan's love for Legos outlasted his brothers' and he continued to ask for Legos for Christmas well into his teens. Yep, he's our artist.

When I look back at Jonathan's unique style of Lego build-ing — improvisational and *sans* instructions, I'm struck by two thoughts. First, he built some really cool things by ignoring the instructions. Second, he never ended up build-ing what was pictured on the front of the box. It didn't matter if his new Lego box was Star Wars themed — he would turn it into a G.I. Joe vehicle. It didn't matter if his new Lego set was intended to build a spaceship — he would build a submarine.

Jonathan has always been a creative, out-of-the-box thinker who constantly looks for new ways to do old things — hence his chronic disregard for instruction manuals.

Unfortunately, I've seen way too many parents approach raising children the way Jonathan approaches Lego construction.

Whether you're a creative anti-instruction type, like Jonathan, or an avid instruction-reader, like William, parenting is *not* at all like building Legos. Why? There are lots of reasons, but the big one that comes to mind is that when we build with Legos, every decision is reversible. The results are always temporary.

On the other hand, when we're building a family, many of the important decisions we make as parents are not reversible. They often leave marks. And the results in our children's lives — for better or for worse — are usually permanent.

> When we're building a family, many of the important decisions we make as parents are not reversible.

Because parental decisions often have long-term and far-reaching effects, it's important that we clearly understand our roles as parents. And it's important we read the instructions. If we want to properly build Lego's Ice Planet, then we must start with the Ice Planet instruction manual. If we want to properly build a godly family, then we must start with the Bible. The Bible is where we find out not only what we're trying to accomplish as parents, but how to actually do it. It's where we find the roles and attitudes we need to embrace in order to raise children who love God with their whole heart.

The Bible isn't a detailed owner's manual with step-by-step instructions for raising kids. But it offers general wisdom and narrates stories of parenting successes and failures from which we can learn valuable lessons.

But if there's one chapter in Scripture that most succinctly summarizes biblical wisdom on the role of parents, I think it's Psalm 127. Only five verses long, it gives the framework for parenting.

The rest of this chapter, we'll take a close look at Psalm 127 and see what it has to say about our roles and attitudes as parents. In other words, these verses describe the heart of the parent. Let's take a look at the roles.

ROLE #1:
PARENTS AS BUILDERS

"Unless the Lord builds the house, those who build it labor in vain. . . ." (Psalm 127:1)

This Scripture mentions two builders. The first is identified as the Lord. While not specifically called parents, the phrase "those who build" refers to parents. This verse makes it clear that the primary role of the parent is to partner with God in building a godly home. Here's what that partnership looks like: we labor and God builds. No one can build a home alone, and no one can build it overnight. Building properly takes time and requires a lot of help.

So what exactly are we building?

Biblical Foundations and Boring Family Devotions
First, we're building spiritual foundations in our children. I'm thankful for Christian schools and dynamic children's ministries and youth groups at church, but ultimately, it's our responsibility as parents to establish spiritual foundations in the lives of our children. For us this involved, among other

things, regular family devotions where we read our children Bible stories and where we attempted to teach them to pray.

Over the years, we attempted a variety of things for family devotions. Some had a great impact. Others seemed like a complete waste of time. We read stories from picture Bibles. We read missionary biographies. One of our favorites was reading through *You Can Change the World*, the kids' version of Patrick Johnstone's missions classic, *Operation World*. If you're unfamiliar with the book *Operation World*, it's like *Wikipedia* for world missions. It has a profile for every country of the world, briefly outlining its spiritual history, its unreached people groups, and its major prayer needs.

> Ultimately, it's our responsibility as parents to establish spiritual foundations in the lives of our children.

We liked reading through *You Can Change the World* because it helped our kids think bigger about God's mission in the world, and it gave us the opportunity to begin praying for the nations with our children. Even though my kids grew up on the mission field, we still thought it was important to intentionally lay the foundation of prayer for all nations. Before they could read, our sons could locate dozens of nations on a map and identify their flags, not because they studied geography, but because our family prayed for the nations together.

Spiritual Subcontractors

Though establishing spiritual foundations is ultimately our parental responsibility, all of us need help. This is where teachers, kids' ministry volunteers, youth pastors, and discipleship group leaders come in. I call these people spiritual subcontractors. They'll never be as important as the parent, but in certain seasons and situations, they can provide valuable help.

About fifteen years ago when our sons were fourteen, twelve, and ten, Deborah and I heard some timely parenting wisdom that really helped us navigate the teen years. I was preaching at Word of Life Church in Red Deer, Alberta, a short drive from the beautiful Canadian Rockies. Word of Life, a Canadian megachurch, was started by my friends Mel and Heather Mullen. Today their son Jachin is the lead pastor, and the church continues to grow locally and globally. Word of Life has always been one of my favorite churches to visit anywhere in the world—not just because of its proximity to Lake Louise and Banff, but because it's such an inspirational and life-giving church.

After the Sunday night service, while eating BBQ with the Mullen family, I asked Mel and Heather how they raised such amazing kids. Their answer really helped Deborah and me. They said, "We got a lot of help!"

When I dug deeper, Mel explained that no matter how hard he and Heather tried to be good parents, they realized they would still need help, especially during the teen years.

I asked where they found parenting help. They responded, "At church. Our kids would not be the adults they are today without help from our kids' ministry teachers, our youth pastors, our associate pastors, our missionaries, and others from our church family who inspired them to give their all to Jesus."

We never forgot that conversation, and from then on, we aggressively sought as much help as we could find. I like to think of our helpers as subcontractors.

As parents, we realize that we're called to be builders, but that doesn't mean we're supposed to do all the building. It means we have the ultimate responsibility and authority.

When my house was built, the builder didn't do everything himself. He hired skilled electricians, plumbers, roofers, painters, and other subcontractors. Like a contractor building a house, parents would be wise to work with subcontractors who have expertise in certain areas.

As I mentioned earlier, Deborah and I found that spiritual subcontractors are especially important in the teen years. For example, when my oldest son was in middle school and high school, he went to Rico Ricafort's discipleship group. Rico was the youth pastor at our church and was way cooler and younger than I was. He was dead serious about obedience to God, biblical moral standards, and spiritual disciplines, but at the same time, he knew how to make life and discipleship feel like a party. Rico was the perfect person to help my son in that season of his development. He was careful to reinforce spiritual foundations in William at a crucial time in his life when he was deciding what he really believed about God, church, and the Bible.

What's important to point out is that Rico was not laying brand new foundations in William. He was building on a foundation that had already been established by Deborah and me. William already knew that the Bible was important, but Pastor Rico inspired him to read it every day. He already knew that sexual purity was important, but Pastor Rico showed him what it looked like for a single man in his twenties to live without a hint of sexual immorality. William already knew that discipleship was important, but Pastor Rico made his discipleship group the most exciting place to be on a Thursday night.

Before William got his driver's license, I used to brave Manila's traffic to pick him up from Rico's group once a week. I would often ask him what they had talked about in discipleship group. Sometimes the lesson was from a published Bible study, sometimes it was based on the Sunday sermon. But more often than not, the lesson sounded oddly similar (try identical) to the one I had discussed in my discipleship group on Thursday mornings, of which Rico was a part.

> Though our role as builders is important, the most important builder in our family is God.

I enjoyed those car rides home, as William would tell me about the awesome lesson Rico had taught them from the Bible (the same lesson which I had taught Rico earlier that day). Somehow I knew that in this season of William's life, those lessons were better received from his youth pastor than directly from his dad. What mattered was that he was excited to read the Bible. What mattered was that the spiritual foundations Deborah and I had been emphasizing for years were now being reinforced by others.

Ultimately, we understood that though our role as builders was important, the most important builder in our family was God. All of our labor as parents was in vain apart from His grace and His activity in our children's lives.

Role #2:
Parents as Guardians

". . . Unless the Lord watches over the city, the watchman stays awake in vain" (Psalm 127:1).

Here's part two of the divine parenting partnership: we guard and God watches over.

The watchmen in Psalm 127 are the parents. The job of a watchman or guard is to watch, discern, warn, protect, and rescue. As guardians and watchmen, parents must be aware of dangerous influences and relationships that could harm their children. Parents must be attentive and discerning, especially regarding friends, music, and extracurricular activities.

In order to explain what it means to watch and guard, read the following questions and see if they can help you assess how you are doing as a spiritual guard in your home:

- Are you aware of the music, TV, and computer games your children listen to, watch, and play?

- Do you have settings on your home internet and mobile devices that filter out pornographic and other harmful websites?

- How well do you know your children's friends and their families?

- Do you always know where your children are and who they're with?

It's important to point out that our role as guardians will look different in different seasons. In other words, the way we monitor our child's media consumption at six years old will look radically different from when he or she is sixteen years old.

For example, when my sons were in elementary school, we closely controlled the movies and television shows they watched to ensure that they weren't prematurely exposed to violent or sexually explicit content. When they were at sleepovers or birthday parties, our sons would often call home and ask if they could watch a certain movie. Usually, the movie was fine, but sometimes Deborah and I would be shocked at what some parents would allow a bunch of adolescent boys to watch.

Our intent was not to insulate them from the outside world, but rather to protect them from absorbing images and values before they were old enough to critically evaluate them according to the Bible.

"Because I Said So"
When they were young, we didn't need to give them a long explanation about why they couldn't watch certain movies or television shows. Short answers, like "It's too violent" or "Because the movie is PG-13 and you're seven" or "Because I said so," were good enough. But when they got into their teen years, answering the "why" question became more important. We wanted to teach them how to think about their media consumption. Our goal was not to raise thoughtless momma's boys who would call us from college and ask if they could watch certain movies. We wanted to teach our sons how to think biblically, rather than blindly following our lead.

In order to effectively fulfill our role as spiritual guardians, as parents, we must find a balance between being overbearing and paranoid, or naive and negligent. Finding the right balance takes wisdom and lots of little adjustments along the way as our children get older and grow in independence.

Sometimes the issue of media consumption can dominate discussions about parenting, and we forget that the friends our children hang out with often can be more influential than what they listen to and watch.

Do you know your kids' friends? Are they a negative or positive influence?

Deborah and I decided to go on the offensive. We cleared our schedules, opened our doors, stocked the pantry, and decided that our home would be a center of activity for our sons and their friends.

It's amazing how quickly children mimic the behavior and attitudes of their peers. You can diligently train your child to act and speak a certain way, and sometimes it can feel like a new group of friends can undo all of that training in a matter of weeks. That's because kids want to be accepted and affirmed by their peers — even if it means rejecting some of the values their parents taught them at home.

The difficulty for parents is that our kids' friends are not like television shows and video games. We can't just turn them off or change the channel. They're neighbors and classmates who will be there tomorrow and the next day. And they're neighbors and classmates who need to hear the gospel of Christ.

So how do we effectively watch over our children's friendships and, at the same time, teach them to befriend people
who need Jesus?

The Best Defense is Good Offense
For Deborah and me, the key was using a combination of
offense and defense. When I say offense, I mean that we
actively tried to bring our sons around kids who we thought
would be a good influence on them. We encouraged these
friendships and made a great effort to support them (by
taking our sons to their birthday parties or inviting them
over to our homes). These friendships usually (but not
always) were formed at church and in youth group.

Even though our sons developed healthy friendships with
people at church, they still had lots of friends from school,
sports teams, and the neighborhood. Most of these friends
were not Christians and some of them weren't the greatest
influence. So how did we play defense? How did we ensure
that a random kid in the neighborhood wasn't being too bad
of an influence on our sons?

As I have said before, every situation is different and requires
wisdom. But Deborah and I decided to go on the offensive.
We cleared our schedules, opened our doors, stocked the
pantry, and decided that our home would be a center of
activity for our sons and their friends. We reasoned that, by
having them on our turf, we could get to know their friends
from the sports teams and neighborhood. Additionally, we
could get to know the families of these kids.

Occasionally, our sons would bring home kids who were cause
for concern. In elementary school, this usually meant kids
with discipline issues. In high school, this meant kids with

attitude issues. When we were concerned about a particular friend or group of friends, we didn't forbid our sons from hanging out with them. Such a drastic approach usually results in the exact opposite effect. But on a few occasions, we did ask our sons about certain friends and the time they were spending with them.

Usually, in those conversations, many of the issues we were concerned about would come up, and it would become clear to our sons that they should be wise about the time they spent with certain friends and aware of the concerns about a given friend's attitude or influence. While these conversations were never easy, they were certainly worth the effort and kept us connected with our sons during their teen years.

Role #3:
Parents as Providers

"It is in vain that you rise up early and go late to rest, eating the bread of anxious toil; for he gives to his beloved sleep" (Psalm 127:2).

At first glance, Psalm 127:2 appears to suggest that working hard to provide for one's family is a pointless endeavor, but what it's actually saying is that our best efforts to provide for our family will ultimately be in vain without God's help.

As I've said before, parenting is a partnership. We labor and God builds. We stand guard and God watches over our families. We work hard and God provides. And though God is the ultimate provider, one of our primary roles as parents is to work hard to provide for our children.

This may seem like the most self-explanatory role in parenting. However, being a provider is more than paying the bills, putting food on the table, and destroying the budget every Christmas. Providing food, shelter, and clothing is important, but it's only the starting point of providing for children. As Christians, our aim is not only to provide physical necessities for our children, but also to model God's generosity towards us as His children.

Do Your Kids Know that God is Generous?

Have you ever thought about God's role as provider for us as His children? God not only provides what we need, He delights in blessing us beyond what we ask so that we can be a blessing to others.

> If you were the only way that your children would learn about who God is as a provider, what would they assume about God?

Is this your mindset when you think about providing for your children? Do you delight in blessing them? Do you model a lifestyle of generosity so that when they're blessed, your children feel the impulse to bless others?

Think about it this way — if you were the only way that your children would learn about who God is as a provider, what would they assume about God? Would their experience in your home cause them to assume that their heavenly Father will joyfully provide all their needs all the time? Would your interactions with your children demonstrate that sometimes God doesn't give us what we want exactly when we want it because He knows what's best for us?

It may seem straightforward — work hard and provide for your family — but our role as provider goes beyond *what* we provide. *How* we provide for our family is just as important as the actual provision.

For example, if we work hard to provide for our children, but constantly complain about how expensive it is to put food on the table, or how much the basketball league entrance fees are, or how hard we had to work to pay the rent — then we aren't only making our children feel like a burden, but we're training them to believe that God sees them that way, too.

If this is the atmosphere in the home, we will make our children feel as if they're a burden to us, rather than a blessing from God. And this will not only make them insecure in their relationship with us, but also in their relationship with their heavenly Father.

You may be tempted to think that the ability to *joyfully* provide is an issue of economics — that somehow wealthy people can afford to pay the bills *with a smile* and poor people can't. But nothing could be further from the truth. I know plenty of wealthy people who complain about the high cost of raising kids, and I know economically poor parents who model God's joy-filled generosity towards their children, even as they struggle to make ends meet. It has nothing to do with actual wealth or poverty. It has everything to do with mentality — a provision mentality or a poverty mentality.

Rejecting a Poverty Mentality

When Deborah and I first moved to the Philippines as missionaries, we had very little money — to the point that we would count our coins before we took a cab and carefully watch the meter so we could ask the cab driver to stop before our fare was more than we had. Needless to say, we did a lot of walking in the early days.

When our children were young, even though we were missionaries with a small church, very little financial support, and lots of vision, we decided that we would never allow a poverty mentality in our family. It didn't matter how little we had; we were determined to be thankful, be generous, and remain confident that our heavenly Father would always provide for our family.

What this meant for our children was that they never heard us complain about how broke we were. They never really knew how little we had because we protected them from our poverty. They never heard us talk about how much food or clothes cost. They never heard us verbalize our anxieties about where the money would come from to pay next month's rent.

This didn't mean that we pretended to be millionaires and gave them everything that they wanted. But it did mean that we joyfully provided all they needed, and we delighted in going beyond their needs and blessing them. Again, this didn't mean buying gifts for our children that we really couldn't afford. And it didn't mean going into credit card debt. It meant lots of praying and creativity.

For example, when William was four and James was two, every Monday on my day off, Deborah and I would take them to V-Mall and buy them new coloring books. James was too young to color, but he did enjoy the colorful wax-like snacks his brother occasionally stuffed into his open mouth when we weren't looking. These Philippine coloring books were cheap and rarely lasted till the next week, but you should have seen William and James's faces every time we took them to the bookstore to pick out that week's coloring book. Their joy was in more than just a new coloring book. Their joy was in their parents' delight. They knew that we enjoyed blessing them. And moments like those prepared them to understand how their heavenly Father delights in blessing them.

Of course, our role as providers also included saying "No"—plenty of times. But we never said, "No, because we can't afford it." Sometimes we could afford it. Often we couldn't. It was a "No, you don't need this right now." You don't need ice cream right now—you need to eat your dinner. You don't need new roller blades right now—you have a perfectly fine pair from Christmas last month. You don't need a sports car for your sixteenth birthday—you need an indestructible armored tank.

Whether we're saying "No," or we're blessing our children with something they never thought to ask for, what we need to understand is that our role as providers isn't just to provide food, shelter, clothing—it's to model God's faithful and joyful generosity towards us.

SEEING CHILDREN
AS GOD SEES THEM

The first half of Psalm 127 (verses 1–2) outlines our roles as parents. Parents are supposed to be builders, guards, and providers. As builders, we partner with God, the master builder. As guardians, we guard, but God watches over our kids. As providers, we work hard, but ultimately God provides.

The second half of Psalm 127 (verses 3–5) highlights three essential attitudes that believers should have towards children. Developing the right attitude is essential to being able to fulfill the roles described in the first two verses.

Attempting to fulfill the roles without the right attitude is the definition of Pharisaical hypocrisy. When parents do the right thing with the wrong attitude, they inadvertently cultivate cynicism and resentment in children.

As we study the heart of parenting, we not only need to look at the heart of every child, we also need to examine our hearts as parents and see if our heart attitudes are the same as God's towards our kids. Here are three essential parental attitudes outlined in Psalm 127. These attitudes show us how God sees children. It's important that we see our children as He sees them.

Parental Attitude #1:
Children Are a Heritage

"Behold, children are a heritage from the Lord . . ." (Psalm 127:3)

The first attitude towards parenting that we find in Psalm 127 needs a little explaining. What does it really mean when it says that children are a "heritage"—or inheritance—from the Lord?

First, inheritances are valuable. The obvious parallel is that children are valuable and to be loved and valued by their parents. But it goes deeper. Inheritances come in all shapes and forms—some things that we inherit are intrinsically valuable (like land or money) and others are only valuable because of who they come from.

For example, as I mentioned in chapter two, one of my prize possessions is a 1959 Rolex from my dad. While the word Rolex suggests great intrinsic value, the watch is a very basic stainless steel Rolex worth much less than an old used car. In fact, I have easily put more money into restoring the watch than it's worth today.

So why is it so valuable to me? It's valuable to me because I was born in 1959, and my dad wore that watch almost every day of my life. I don't remember a day when he wasn't wearing it. He wore it to work. He wore it to baseball practice. He wore it to fish. He wore it to garden. It never left his wrist (which explains why it needed so much restoration when I got it).

So when he passed away in 2002, I asked my brothers and sisters if I could have his watch. Why? I didn't want it so I could sell it and buy something else. I didn't want it for its monetary value. It was valuable to me because of who it came from.

In the same way, our children have value because God gave them to us.

It doesn't matter if anyone outside of your family recognizes the value of your children. Their primary value is not in their future success or their potential benefit to us—they are valuable because they're a gift from God.

This brings us to my second point. Inheritances aren't earned. They're gifts. The only thing that qualifies us to inherit is being born into a certain family. We can't work or will ourselves into an inheritance. It all depends on family.

If we extend this idea towards children and parenting, we realize that we have done nothing to earn the right to be parents. God freely gives us children because we are His children. They're a gift, not a right. And they're ultimately God's — not ours.

So here's the question: Do you see your children as a valuable inheritance from God?

PARENTAL ATTITUDE #2: CHILDREN ARE A REWARD

"Behold, children are a heritage from the Lord, the fruit of the womb a reward" (Psalm 127:3).

The second attitude towards children that we find in Psalm 127 is very closely related to the first attitude. If we view children as an inheritance, it'll be natural to see them as a reward.

So often in our success-driven culture, children are seen as an unwanted responsibility, a financial burden, or an impediment to one's career. So prevalent is this view that over one million abortions are conducted every year in the United States alone. Think about how different those numbers would be if every parent saw children as rewards from God. It's unthinkable that anyone would throw away a reward.

> It doesn't matter if anyone outside of your family recognizes the value of your children. Their primary value is not in their future success or their potential benefit to us — they are valuable because they're a gift from God.

Why are millions of rewards from God rejected? Because many people don't view children as a reward but as an accident, a mistake, or a burden.

Even Christians sometimes accept their role as parents begrudgingly, longing for the day when their children grow up and pay their own bills. It's true that children are expensive. It's true that children demand time. And it's true that becoming a parent requires supernatural patience and cataclysmic lifestyle changes.

This is all true. But if we learn to see children as God sees them—as rewards—then all of the expense, time, and lifestyle changes will pale in comparison to the rewards of parenthood.

You may feel like you've sacrificed a lot for your children. You have. At times you may even feel that they're more of a burden than a blessing. I know many amazing parents whose children have brought them much heartache. But regardless of our parenting ups and downs and regardless of how our children have turned out so far, if we embrace God's attitude towards children, in the long run, we'll find that they're a reward worth far more than all the invisible sacrifices that we constantly make for them.

PARENTAL ATTITUDE #3: CHILDREN ARE LIKE ARROWS

"Like arrows in the hand of a warrior are the children of one's youth. Blessed is the man who fills his quiver with them!" (Psalm 127:4–5)

The final thing we learn in Psalm 127 is the idea that children, like arrows, are not meant to stay in the quiver—their purpose is to be aimed and released towards a target. Because most people in our culture don't own a "real bow and arrow," we miss out on half of the metaphor. So, bear with me as I attempt to explain the context of arrows and quivers.

The original audience of this psalm probably would have been familiar with the process of arrow-making. People in the ancient Near East didn't just go to the ammo store to buy their arrows. They painstakingly made them by hand. First, they selected a straight branch of wood. Next, they stripped off all the twigs and leaves. Then, they sanded the arrow till it was straight and smooth. Finally, they sharpened the point. Then, and only then, was the arrow ready to go in the quiver.

There wasn't a shortcut for the process. No matter how skilled the archer, an arrow that wasn't straight and smooth would never hit the target. And an arrow that wasn't razor-sharp wouldn't penetrate the target. In a society where people hunted for their food, no one could afford to have crooked and dull arrows. Having a quiver full of good arrows was vital to survival.

As important as it was for hunters in the ancient Near East to handcraft straight and sharp arrows before they put them in their quiver, it's also important for us to raise our children with great care and intentionality.

While I know I'm in danger of pushing a good metaphor into an allegory, it's safe to say that the key stages of arrow-making have interesting parallels with parenting. In the same way that archers strip the leaves and twigs off the branch and sand it smooth, parents also need to work on the rough edges of their children's character and remove bad habits and attitudes that might cause them to veer off-course. In the same way that archers sharpen the arrow to have a razor-sharp point, parents should also equip their children with the skills and disciplines necessary to be effective in their future calling.

Do you have the attitude of an archer in the way that you raise your children? Are you raising them with the reality in mind that one day, they'll be aimed and released at a target?

Some parents lack intentionality in their parenting. In other words, their quiver is full of rough, crooked, and dull arrows—and they don't even realize it. They don't see the importance of preparing their children for the future. They just assume that when they release the arrow, wherever the wind takes it will be okay.

> Children, like arrows, are meant to be handcrafted and eventually released. If they're not crafted well, they won't shoot straight. And if they aren't released, they'll never hit their target.

Other parents are very intentional in their parenting, but they forget that arrows aren't meant to stay in the quiver. In fact, it's often the parents who take great care in raising their children who have the hardest time releasing them from the quiver into adulthood. After all the time and care they put into raising them, blinded by well-meaning fear, they keep their adult "kids" close and safely hidden in the quiver.

Both ends of the extreme miss the point.

Different Arrows, Different Targets

Children, like arrows, are meant to be handcrafted and eventually released. If they're not crafted well, they won't shoot straight. And if they aren't released, they'll never hit their target.

When our three sons were still in our house, we worked hard to shape their character, and we also worked hard to equip them with valuable life skills so they would one day be sharp and effective in whatever God called them to do.

Every child is different and has unique gifts and callings. And while our children are in our home, we need to see them as arrows that we are handcrafting and preparing for release. We want to work on their character so they'll fly straight. We want to equip them so they'll be sharp. And we want to release them so they'll hit the unique target that God has prepared for them, rather than spending their lives in the safety of the quiver.

SEASONS OF WAR AND PEACE IN THE HOME

In 1812, Napoleon and friends invaded Russia. Immediately, Tsar Alexander declared war on France. In 1986, our first son was born, ending years of peace and sleep in our lives. His birth was a declaration of war on our normal.

In the next few decades, we fought many wars — winning some, losing some, and declaring a tie in others. Looking back, I realize that sometimes we were fighting the wrong battles, but at least we were fighting rather than retreating, deserting, or pretending that everything was fine.

Here are two battles I'm glad we fought, no matter how long they lasted and no matter how bloody they got: spiritual battles that made an impact on our sons' relationship with

God, and relational battles that made an impact on their connection with us and with one another.

We didn't fight battles that pertained to hair length, clothing styles, music preferences, sports, and other skirmishes that parents often fight and win. We didn't because often, in doing so, parents lose something more important than the trivial turf they're defending.

If we fight and win the wars that matter, then we will experience long seasons of peace in the home.

DISCUSSION QUESTIONS

1. Of the three biblical roles of parents (from Psalm 127)—builder, guardian, and provider—which do you find the most challenging to fulfill? Why?

2. Have you ever thought about your children as your inheritance and a reward? How can this biblical (and countercultural) attitude change the way you parent? Be specific.

3. Have you ever thought about your children as arrows? How can this powerful metaphor change the way you parent? Be specific.

7

JOURNEY TO
THE CENTER OF THE EARTH
Five Deadly Heart Issues

While there is life there is hope. As long as a man's heart beats, as long as a man's flesh quivers, I do not allow that a being gifted with thought and will can allow himself to despair.

Jules Verne, *Journey to the Center of the Earth*

"And he will turn the hearts of fathers to their children and the hearts of children to their fathers..."

Malachi 4:6

Keep your heart with all vigilance, for from it flow the springs of life.

Proverbs 4:23

Every parent has those days when they feel like a complete failure. For several years, Sunday was that day for Deborah and me. When I say Sunday, I mean every Sunday!

For a few years, it seemed like every single Sunday, a children's ministry volunteer would sheepishly approach me after the service. I knew they didn't want to start the conversation, so I would make it a little easier on them: "What did Jonathan do today?"

In those days, our youngest son, sweet and huggable Jonathan, was the terror of children's church. Picking on girls. Dancing on tables during worship. Eating other kids' snacks. Sometimes the reports from children's ministry volunteers made me mad, sometimes they made me laugh, and sometimes they made me feel like a failure as a parent.

I was the pastor. I was supposed to know how to be a good parent. I was supposed to have perfect kids, right?

JOURNEY TO THE HEART OF THE ISSUE

If biblical wisdom on parenting is simple enough to be summed up in the five verses of Psalm 127, then why do so many Christian parents—even pastors—struggle to raise their children? Why do we sometimes fail as builders, watchmen, and providers?

> Whether we like it or not, if we want to parent our children's hearts, we must first examine deep issues in our own hearts.

Why does it sometimes feel like the arrows that we so carefully crafted, aimed, and released are now flying full speed towards the wrong target?

We can do everything right (relatively speaking), and sometimes, our children still rebel in certain seasons of their lives. Sometimes circumstances outside of our control can have negative and long-term effects on our children's lives.

But like it or not, sometimes the problems stem directly from us as parents. Even if we embrace our roles as builders, watchmen, and providers, and even if we see our children as a heritage, a reward, and sharp arrows, certain heart issues can undermine our success as parents.

In Jules Verne's classic, *Journey to the Center of the Earth*, Professor Lidenbrock, an astonishingly fearless and endlessly inquisitive character, drags his reluctant and fearful nephew Alex along with him on his fantastic journey. Along the way, they pick up a third companion, Hans, as their guide. Professor Lidenbrock believed that if they descended a certain volcano in Iceland at a certain time of the year — when the shadows were just right — they would find a volcanic crater shaft that would take them to the center of the earth. A journey like that is rife with fear, pain, and danger, and few are willing to attempt the descent.

> Everything that we do as parents is simply an overflow of what is stored in our hearts.

Like descending a volcano shaft to go to the center of the earth, digging deep into the issues of the heart can be dangerous and sometimes painful. Few of us really want to go there. Most of us need people in our lives like Professor Lidenbrock, who will encourage, push, or force us to go where we're afraid to go on our own. Whether we like it or not, if we want to parent our children's hearts, we must first examine deep issues in our own hearts.

In Proverbs 4:23, we're reminded by Solomon to "keep your heart with all vigilance, for from it flow the springs of life." In other words, everything that we do as parents is simply an overflow of what is stored in our hearts. Our words, our actions, our approach to discipline, our work as builders, watchmen, and providers — they all flow from the heart. And if we don't guard our heart against certain destructive attitudes and tendencies, we will find that everything we do as parents suffers.

I fly a lot, so I know some of the Delta Airlines staff better than I know my neighbors. Every time I fly, I hear a variation of the same safety announcement:

> In the unlikely event of a drop in cabin pressure, panels above your seat will open, revealing oxygen masks. If this happens, pull a mask towards you until the tube is fully extended, place the mask over your nose and mouth. Breathe normally. (I'm always thankful they remind me to breathe.)

> If you're traveling with a child, be sure to adjust your own mask before helping others.

That last sentence is particularly pertinent to parenting — especially the parent's heart.

Wise airline safety advice: adjust your own mask before attempting to adjust your child's mask.

Wise parental safety advice: adjust your own heart before attempting to adjust your child's heart.

The tricky thing is that many of our own heart issues are difficult to detect and can manifest themselves in different ways as we try to fulfill our biblical roles as parents. Ultimately, these heart issues require us to examine ourselves regularly and allow the Holy Spirit to convict and transform us.

Even after we embrace the biblical roles and attitudes towards parenting we discussed in the previous chapter, it's vitally important that we guard our hearts against the following five deadly diseases that can undermine our efforts as parents: legalism, compromise, favoritism, passivity, and idolatry.

LEGALISM: HOW TO RAISE PHARISEES AND REBELS

In the minds of many people in our society, legalism and Christian parenting are synonymous. Simply add the adjective "Christian" when talking about "parenting" and people assume this inevitably results in more rules, steeper consequences, less freedom for the child, lame music, and outdated clothes.

While it's true that legalism plagues many Christian families, I believe that legalism is antithetical to biblical parenting. It totally misses the heart of parenting and undermines our work as builders, watchmen, and providers—or simply as parents.

What does legalism look like? It's tempting to simply list a bunch of stereotypical examples.

- The parents who won't let their children watch any movies that are PG-13—even if the film is Mark Burnett's *Son of God*.

- The parents who only let their children listen to "Christian" music—regardless of the actual message of the songs or the lifestyle of the singers.

- The parents who won't let their son grow long hair — even though we all know (from the movies) that Jesus had long hair and the first mention of a haircut in the Bible caused God's power and presence to depart from Samson.

But in reality, legalism is less about the quantity (or absurdity) of the rules that parents set for their children and more about the importance parents place on the rules themselves. The purpose of setting rules and boundaries is to protect children from things that will harm them, to teach them self-governance, and to develop self-control. But well-intentioned boundary-setting can quickly turn to legalism if we forget that rules are about protecting and teaching, and begin treating them as a measure of acceptance and a means of control.

We've all witnessed it before: two sets of parents adopt identical behavioral guidelines for their children with completely opposite results. Why? Because one family was loving and gracious and the other family was mired in legalism. The quantity or severity of the rules is not the primary issue. The real difference between legalism and grace in parenting is the purpose behind the rules. As soon as your children see rule-keeping as a means of gaining your acceptance rather than a means of protection, you've crossed the line into legalism. And as soon as rule-setting becomes more about controlling external behavior than teaching internal self-governance, you're slipping into legalism.

The Unintended Results of Legalism

What does legalism do to a family? If parents consistently place an undue emphasis on rule-keeping and make children feel like parental love and acceptance hinges on their ability to keep rules, then we'll produce either arrogant Pharisees or angry rebels. Legalistic parenting produces Pharisees when children make great efforts to earn their parents' acceptance by strictly following all of the rules. These children may look really good from the outside (and often make their parents look good too), but behind the spotless record and impressive accomplishments, we often find individuals who are prideful, insecure, and judgmental.

Legalistic parenting also produces rebels. This happens when children finally reject the legalistic game—often after repeated failure to measure up to their parents' standards—and decide that it's not worth the trouble to earn their parents' acceptance. So rather than striving to keep every legalistic rule like a Pharisee, the rebel will often intentionally break as many rules as possible.

> As soon as your children see rule-keeping as a means of gaining your acceptance rather than a means of protection, you've crossed the line into legalism.

While many parents would rather have a Pharisee who is on the honor roll than a rebel who's flunking school, both conditions are equally deadly. And both conditions result from legalism in the home. With the Pharisee, we have a kid who believes the only way to earn Mom and Dad's acceptance, and ultimately God's acceptance, is by working really hard. With the rebel, we have someone who finally decides that having a relationship with parents, and ultimately with God, is just not worth the trouble.

So how do we avoid legalism as parents? How do we guard our hearts against this destructive condition? Three ways.

First, as parents, we need a deep revelation of the gospel. We need to understand that our relationship with God is not based on our religious performance, but on Jesus' vicarious sacrifice. We're not accepted because of what we do for God, but because of what God did for us. Our relationship is not based on our commitment to Him, but on His commitment to us.

Second, we can take a simple cue from Paul in Colossians 3:21 when he says, "Fathers, do not provoke your children, lest they become discouraged." Harsh, legalistic parenting that emphasizes rule-keeping over relationship will certainly embitter and discourage our children. What's worse, it will deeply affect the way they relate with their heavenly Father.

Finally, we must understand that our children need to know that we love and accept them regardless of their performance. So though we do need to celebrate good grades and excellence in sports and music, we especially need to express our love and acceptance to our children when they fail. Bad grades. Missed free throws. Painful piano recitals. Do your kids know in those moments of failure that you love and accept them anyway?

COMPROMISE: HOW TO BECOME A JOKE TO YOUR CHILDREN

One of the saddest verses in the Bible has to be Genesis 19:14. Here's the context. God sent angels to warn Lot of the pending destruction of Sodom and Gomorrah. He has little time, so he quickly goes to warn his family: "So Lot went out and said to his sons-in-law, who were to marry his daughters,

'Up! Get out of this place, for the Lord is about to destroy the city.' But he seemed to his sons-in-law to be jesting."

What a tragic scene. Lot is communicating the most urgent matters of life and death to his family, and they think that he's joking.

Why did his adult daughters and their fiancés not take him seriously? How could he have so little credibility with his family?

Good questions. Simple answer: Compromise.

Lot's life, up until this point, was characterized by compromise and a lack of personal integrity. Here's the short version of the sad story of Lot. He had traveled to Canaan with Abraham, his uncle. The Genesis story repeatedly tells us that Abraham followed God, and that Lot followed Abraham. The obvious lesson is that it's not enough to follow a relative who follows God.

> Our children need to know that we love and accept them regardless of their performance.

While in the Promised Land, Abraham and Lot's herders began to quarrel over grazing rights. So Abraham gave Lot the first choice of where to move, and in Genesis 13:12, we learn that "Abram settled in the land of Canaan, while Lot settled among the cities of the valley and moved his tent as far as Sodom." The writer of Genesis, aware of the danger in this move, writes, "Now the men of Sodom were wicked, great sinners against the Lord" (Genesis 13:13). So given the choice of where to live, Lot moved his family near Sodom — a city known for wickedness and depravity, because it seemed to be the better financial move.

Incremental Compromise

The next time we hear about Lot (Genesis 14:12), we find out that he is "dwelling in Sodom" and that he has gotten caught up in a regional war between Sodom and some neighboring kingdoms. In the course of the war, Lot and his family are captured by the enemy, prompting Uncle Abraham to rescue him.

You'd think that Lot would learn his lesson and stay away from Sodom. But he doesn't. The next time we hear about Lot (Genesis 19:1), "Lot was sitting in the gate of Sodom." In the ancient Near East, the gateway not only represented the physical entrance to the city, but it was a place where city leaders gathered to discuss important matters concerning the community. In short, Lot went from living near Sodom to living in Sodom to being an important community leader who sat "in the gate of Sodom." While community involvement can be a great thing, Lot's physical movement towards Sodom seems to have corresponded with a heart movement away from God.

It's important to understand that Lot's compromise was incremental. Lot knew about God, and he saw firsthand the results of Abraham's faith in God's promise. In 1 Peter, he's even referred to as a "righteous man." But instead of staying with Abraham in the Promised Land, Lot chose the comforts of Sodom—not realizing that his compromises would destroy his credibility and his family. Unfortunately, it's common for righteous men and women to gradually compromise, inadvertently destroying their families.

While Lot was a respected man in the city, he had lost all credibility at home. The Bible gives us few details on his relationships with his wife and daughters, but one story in Genesis 19 gives us some insight into why Lot's wife and daughters had no respect for him.

In Genesis 19, we learn that the angels who warned Lot about the destruction of Sodom and Gomorrah stayed in his home. And late that night, men from the city surrounded the house and demanded that Lot give up his guests, so they could rape them. (Clearly they didn't realize that Lot's houseguests were actually angels.) Lot refused to give up his guests, but instead of sending the mob away, he said, "Behold, I have two daughters who have not known any man. Let me bring them out to you, and do to them as you please" (Genesis 19:8). This is the lunatic fringe of hospitality.

You may be thinking: "What a terrible father! I would never do something like that." Fair enough.

But I imagine that Lot would have never thought he'd get to that point either. That's just the nature of compromise. We begin with small compromises, and eventually, we find ourselves making decisions that not only undermine our credibility with our family but also put our children and our spouse in harm's way. Compromise clouds the mind and makes crazy solutions seem rational. And often, underneath the compromise, there is a sick desire to be respected by peers — even if it destroys family.

Lordship Crushes Compromise
For those who struggle with compromise, the root issue is a lack of Lordship. If Jesus is Lord, then we'll value what He values, and we'll value family the way He values family. If He's not Lord, then our energy will be spent trying to impress all the wrong people.

What's worse, not only will we lose credibility with our children, but our inconsistency of character will cause them to believe that God is inconsistent and can't be trusted.

So how do we deal with compromise in our own hearts?

It starts with Lordship and complete surrender to Jesus. But it doesn't end there. We need to have healthy relationships in our lives. We all need mentors who can model what good parents look like, and peers who can see through our facades and call out our small areas of compromise before they destroy our family.

Are you transparent with anyone in your life? Do you allow them to be honest with you? Do you have a friend who will warn you when it appears you're gradually inching towards Sodom?

FAVORITISM: HOW TO MAKE YOUR CHILDREN HATE EACH OTHER

In certain cultures, favoritism in families is expected.

I can't tell you how many times I've introduced my three boys to new people at church, only to be asked the question: "Which one is your favorite?"

My usual response was simple, "William is my favorite first-born. James is my favorite middle son. And Jonathan is my favorite youngest."

Coming from a different culture, my wife and I were always shocked by this question. I used to think that only Filipinos played favorites with their children, but after spending more time in the United States, I've come to realize that Americans play favorites too. They're just more subtle about it.

Whether we make it painfully public or never articulate it, our children will know if we have a favorite, and they'll suffer the unintended consequences.

They'll notice if we spend more time with one of our children than the others. They'll notice if we discipline unevenly, letting the favorite off the hook. They'll notice if we attend every sports event of one child and regularly miss the piano recitals of the other. They'll notice if we're more generous towards the favorite than the others.

> Not only will we lose credibility with our children, but our inconsistency of character will cause them to believe that God is inconsistent and can't be trusted.

What are the results?

Favoritism produces two equally destructive roots in the heart of every child. For the favorite, a deep sense of entitlement, and for the non-favored, a deep sense of insecurity. What's more, favoritism causes serious alienation among siblings, making it difficult for them to develop healthy friendships as brothers and sisters.

Favoritism Destroys Families
In the Bible, we find several families that were destroyed by favoritism. Think about Isaac's family. Isaac favored Esau, while his wife, Rebekah, favored Jacob.

What happened? Rebekah convinced Isaac to steal his older brother's birthright and the two brothers were alienated for decades. (See Genesis 25-27.)

You would think that Jacob would learn his lesson, but he played favorites with his children too. He had twelve sons and one daughter, and his favorites were Joseph and Benjamin. His favoring of Joseph was so obvious that he gave him a special coat that he didn't give to his other sons. What was the result? In Genesis 37:4, we read, "But when his brothers saw that their father loved him [Joseph] more than all his brothers, they hated him and could not speak peacefully to him." They hated Joseph so much that they contemplated killing him and ultimately ended up selling him into slavery.

This is what happens when we play favorites with our children. Perhaps they won't sell their sibling into slavery, but they will certainly experience alienation and deep insecurity. What do you expect? If our actions show that we love one more than the others — even if we never say it — the others will always wonder why they're not good enough to be worthy of their parents' love.

Favoritism in the home cultivates a performance mentality among children. In other words, by picking favorites, we're teaching our children to compete with each other for parental attention and love. We're teaching them that love and acceptance can be earned only if they can get good-enough grades, or make the basketball team, or achieve success in whatever arbitrary areas we deem important.

What's worse, if we play favorites with our children, we'll teach them to believe that God also plays favorites. And nothing could be further from the truth.

All throughout the Bible, we're reminded that God doesn't show favoritism. We shouldn't either. (See Acts 10:34; Romans 2:11; Galatians 2:6; Ephesians 6:9; Colossians 3:25; 1 Timothy 5:21; James 2:1.)

What's at the heart of favoritism in families? And how can we avoid it?

How to Avoid Favoritism

First, we need to understand that God doesn't play favorites in His family. Nothing we can do will make Him love us any more or any less. He loves us with an unconditional, radical love that's not based on our performance but on the righteousness of Jesus. When He sees us, He sees His Son, with whom He is "well pleased." (See Matthew 3:17 and 17:5.)

Second, we need to go out of our way to treat our children fairly. Sometimes we may not realize it, but something we did or said causes one of our children to think that we

> By picking favorites, we're teaching our children to compete with each other for parental attention and love.

love him or her less than the others. Children want to know that their parents love them just as much as their siblings, and they'll naturally notice any apparent inequity.

For Deborah and me, this meant that we spent exactly the same amount of money on our sons' Christmas gifts and birthday parties. Deborah was so passionate about not having any semblance of favoritism that if one of their Christmas gifts cost five dollars less than the others, she would give one a five dollar cash "balance." I think the boys always appreciated that we went out of our way to show that they were all our favorites.

When William graduated from high school, we decided to give him a mechanical Swiss watch. (I was raised to believe that if it has a battery, it doesn't belong on a man's wrist.) So what did that mean for James and Jonathan? You guessed it; they got watches of comparable value when they graduated from high school. It didn't matter who got a higher GPA when they graduated. They were our sons, and we went out of our way to make sure they were treated equally.

Our middle son, James, caught on rather quickly, and soon began to plan far in advance what he would ask for at certain milestones (based on what William received). So when he was a sophomore in high school, he started looking at watches.

Do all of your children know that you love them unconditionally and equally? Or do you play favorites?

PASSIVITY: HOW TO AVOID DECISIONS THAT MATTER

Believe it or not, playing favorites is not the only guaranteed way to make children deeply insecure. Passivity will do it too.

What do I mean by passivity? What does it look like to be a passive parent? The most obvious manifestation of passivity is a lack of leadership in the home and a lack of engagement in our children's lives. A lack of leadership at home affects both big decisions, like where to attend church, and small decisions, like where to eat lunch after church. Passive parents choose the path of least resistance — avoiding both important and insignificant decisions that can make an impact on the family.

Here's a practical example: education. What went into your decision about where your children would go to school? I'm consistently shocked by how little thought often goes into this massive decision. Not only is the quality of our children's education hugely important, but the environment that they're educated in is equally important.

So many parents passively assume that because they live in a certain neighborhood or school district, their children will go to a particularly good school. Maybe. But have you looked into the school? Does it have excellent teachers and staff, and does it produce quality students? Is it a safe place for children, or is it known for crime and drug use? While I understand that economics factor into decisions about schools, it's not an excuse to be passive about this decision.

Before I go on, let me make myself clear. I'm not an advocate for a one-size-fits-all family education policy. Some people claim that homeschooling is best. Others claim that Christian schools are best. Some prefer expensive prep schools. And others prefer free public schools. In my years as a parent and pastor, I've seen countless examples of each of those types of schools working wonderfully—and sometimes terribly—for parents and kids. What matters most is making the best decisions for your children based on your family's unique context.

Even if you can't afford the school you really want for your children, you have plenty of options. Some people homeschool. Some people move to a different part of town to be in a better school district. Some people apply for scholarships.

You'll have more options than you can imagine if you'll take this decision seriously and take it to God in prayer.

Even if you can afford any school for your children, don't quickly assume that the best place for your child is the expensive private school. It doesn't matter if all your friends and colleagues send their kids to a particular school. Do your research. Pray through your options. Think about what's best for your children, both in regard to education and environment.

Emotionally Engaged Parenting

Another sign of passive parenting is a lack of engagement with children. Are you involved in their lives? Do you ask questions about their day at school? Do you coach their sports teams? Do you eat dinner together as a family? Do you show up for the things that matter to them?

Sometimes, a lack of parental engagement stems from busyness at work, but other times it's simply a lack of intentionality. Sure, life gets busy. Sure, teenagers don't like opening up. Sure, it can be easier to watch TV as a family than to actually talk. Passive parents allow things like busyness, teen angst, and a new TV show to deter them from really engaging their children.

So how do we engage? How can we avoid being the parent who lives with their children, but doesn't really know what's going on in their lives?

First, we need to make time for our children — whether that means adjusting work hours in order to be at baseball practice or spending time with them when you get home from work.

Second, we need to make space for meaningful engagement with our children. Not all time spent together is equally meaningful. A meaningful relational connection doesn't happen just because the whole family is in the car together on the way to church. For our family, dinner became a place for meaningful engagement. Every weeknight, we all sat down together for dinner. We had a strict no TV, no phones policy. We also had a no eat-and-run policy.

> Our children knew that no matter how busy the day was with school, work, tennis practice, or homework, we would set those things aside for dinner.

Everyone sat down together for dinner. No one left the table until everyone was finished. In the meantime, we talked. And laughed. And told stories. And argued (sports and politics). And laughed some more.

Our children knew that no matter how busy the day was with school, work, tennis practice, or homework, we would set those things aside for dinner. At dinner, we would talk about our day. We would talk about the kids' sports teams. We would talk about things going on at school. Our sons would talk, and Deborah and I would listen. Nothing profound. No ministry moments. Just screenless family time.

Parents can find many ways to engage their children, but strategies vary depending on age, family size, and the season of life. What matters is that we make time and space for meaningful engagement.

Parents who lead their families well don't use remote control autopilot parenting. They thoughtfully and prayerfully lead and engage their children. We found that the best way to engage our children was by asking good questions. As our sons got older, these questions became the catalyst for some great mealtime discussions. (Caution: I'm not talking about the questions of a religious inquisition, but the questions of an interested parent who actually trusts the child and cares about the big and little events and emotions of the day.)

> When we consistently prioritize work over family, we're showing what's really in our heart. We're showing what matters to us most.

Great parents ask good questions. Then they listen without interrupting, condemning, or sermonizing. Ask and listen. You'll be amazed at what you learn about your kids.

IDOLATRY: HOW TO LOSE WHAT MATTERS MOST

Some parents' passivity and lack of engagement stems from not having good examples or courage, but some parents are just too busy with work to be engaged in the lives of their children.

In many scenarios, both parents have to work in order to pay the bills, but this should never be an excuse to neglect children.

Truth be told, most of my workaholic friends whose work always seems to take priority over their kids are not people who struggle to pay the bills. They're usually very successful and very motivated—so motivated that they forget about the things that matter most. Sadly, this is sometimes even the case with pastors and missionaries.

I know way too many people in ministry who have sacrificed their children on the altar of ministerial success. In their efforts to save the world, they end up losing their family. Make no mistake about it. The Bible calls this idolatry. It doesn't matter whether we get our priorities wrong as a lawyer or pastor. It's still idolatry because we have made a good thing (work) a god thing. When we consistently prioritize work over family, we're showing what's really in our heart. We're showing what matters to us most.

Those of us in ministry can convince themselves that since we're doing "the Lord's work," it's okay for us to miss our son's baseball game or our daughter's tennis match. Or since we're caring for the spiritual well-being of the entire church, it's okay for us to sacrifice time with our own family. What a tragic and all-too-common deception.

How do we avoid ministry idolatry? How do we avoid prioritizing work over family?

We can learn from the example of Noah. In Genesis 7:1, we read, "Then the Lord said to Noah, 'Go into the ark, you and all your household . . .'" And in Hebrews 11:7, "By faith Noah, being warned by God concerning events as yet unseen, in reverent fear constructed an ark for the saving of his household."

Family was central to Noah's mission.

Noah's family was not a distraction. It wasn't a side issue. It was, in many ways, the central issue. God had called Noah to save the world. But God didn't tell Noah to load a bunch of strangers and animals on the boat and then see if he had enough room for his family. God planned to save the world through Noah and his family.

ARKS AND ROW BOATS: HOW TO RECOGNIZE WHAT MATTERS

Can you imagine what would have happened if Noah prioritized the "mission" over his family instead of realizing that they were inextricably connected? Or can you imagine what would have happened if Noah lost his credibility with his family (like Lot) and couldn't convince his family to get on the boat?

I realize that some people idolize family, but not nearly as many as those who idolize success, career, and ministry. The sin of family idolatry is basically building a family-centered life rather than a Christ-centered life, a child-centered home rather than a Christ-centered home, a principle-centered child rather than a Christ-centered child. He may be a well-mannered, home-schooled, Bible-quoting ten-year-old, but if he's the center of your life rather than Christ, he's still an idol.

What the Right Heart Can Produce

In contrast to the five deadly heart issues that can destroy family, here's a story that illustrates what the right heart can produce.

Many people remember the 1924 Summer Olympics in Paris as the summer when Scottish sprinter and Olympic favorite Eric Liddell withdrew from the one-hundred-meter dash because it fell on the Sabbath. As we all know from the 1981 Oscar-winning movie, *Chariots of Fire*, his sacrifice was vindicated when he shocked the world by winning the gold medal in the 400-meter race a few days later.

While Liddell's sacrifice was remarkable and *Chariots of Fire* is one of my favorite movies, it doesn't compare to the sacrifice made in the same summer by Bill Havens.

Havens was on the United States Olympic rowing team in 1924. His team was heavily favored to win gold medals in both the individual and team rowing events. Havens was one of the best rowers on the team, but after much deliberation, he decided not to go to Paris with the team.

Why?

Because months before the Olympics, Havens found out that his wife was pregnant and that their first baby would be due during the Olympics. Though the Olympic competition would last only two weeks, Havens lived in a time before commercial air travel. In those days, people crossed the Atlantic on steamships (think Titanic). Two weeks from New York to London, plus two weeks of competition, followed by two weeks from London to New York. He would be away a minimum of six weeks. In other words, if Havens went to Paris for the Olympics, it would be impossible to get back to the United States in time for the birth of his child.

After spending several days agonizing over the decision and after seeking counsel from close friends and family (all of whom told him that he should go to Paris), Havens decided to skip the Olympics in order to be next to his wife when his child was born.

On August 1, 1924, four days after the official end of the summer games, Bill's wife gave birth to a son they named Frank.

Many years later, Bill Havens questioned whether or not skipping the Olympics was the right decision. Several of his teammates had won gold medals in Paris. It could have been and should have been Bill's gold. Bill never made it back to the Olympics and never won his gold medal. He was tormented by this question for nearly three decades — until he received a telegram from Helsinki, Finland, the site of the 1952 Summer Olympics. It read, "Dear Dad, Thanks for waiting around for me to get born in 1924. I'm coming home with the gold medal you should have won. Your loving son, Frank."

It's natural for parents to want their children to be more successful than they were. Bill Havens dreamed of Olympic gold. But he sacrificially prioritized his family more than his dream. The son achieved the gold that the father only dreamed about achieving. This true story about preparing our children for greatness poignantly captures the heart of parenting.

Writing about the next generation of spiritual sons and daughters, the apostle John penned these words, "I have no greater joy than to hear that my children are walking in the truth" (3 John 1:4).

As a parent, I experienced great joy when my sons hit home runs, won tennis trophies, made straight As, created beautiful art, wrote great songs, and exhibited Christian character. But nothing compares to the joy of knowing that they're walking with God and walking in truth.

DISCUSSION QUESTIONS

1. How did legalism, compromise, favoritism, passivity, and idolatry affect your home growing up?

2. Of the five deadly heart issues — legalism, favoritism, compromise, passivity, and idolatry—which ones do you most often find in your own heart? How does it affect the way you parent?

3. How can the truth of the gospel transform your heart and make you a better parent?

8

THE PILGRIM'S PROGRESS
Disappointment and Broken Hearts

Saint abroad, and a devil at home.
John Bunyan, *The Pilgrim's Progress*

Saying and doing are two things indeed, and are as diverse, as are the Soul and the Body.
John Bunyan, *The Pilgrim's Progress*

And I am sure of this, that he who began a good work in you will bring it to completion at the day of Jesus Christ.
Philippians 1:6

That's not how we raised you."

My sons have heard that phrase a million times. When they acted selfishly with a new toy, when they complained about household chores, when they practiced piano half-heartedly, when they slammed a tennis racket on the ground after a double fault, when their tone was disrespectful, they always heard, "That's not how we raised you."

I have to confess that, as adults, they still occasionally hear it. And it makes them laugh. They laugh and remind us that we also had a companion phrase that was the flip side of "That's not how we raised you."

The other phrase was spoken every time William, James, or Jonathan did something that made us proud. When they brought home straight As, when they lost a tennis match graciously, when they won humbly, when they ate their vegetables, when they said "Thank you," when they shared their toys, they always heard, "That's how we raised you."

My sons think it's so funny that Deborah and I take credit for all their successes and blame them for all their failures. Their successes are because of how we raised them, and their failures are because they're not acting according to how we raised them. Deborah and I laugh along with them as we try to explain that it's a universal parental prerogative to take credit for the greatness of our kids (and to disavow familial relations when they mess up).

From Fame to Shame

Our good friends Aaron and Susan (not their real names) once told us a funny story about their pre-teen son, Billy (not his real name). One bright and sunny day Billy shocked his parents by bringing home a perfect report card. Of course, that's exactly how Aaron and Susan raised him! And they praised and honored him accordingly.

Sometimes life as a parent is perfect.

A week later, they caught Billy lying. That was not how they raised him. As Aaron patiently and calmly engaged his son in a fatherly conversation about truth and integrity, Susan's patience was wearing thin. When she reached the end of her rope, she pointed her finger in Billy's face and emphatically said, "We were so proud last week; now we're so disappointed. In just one week you've gone from fame to shame!" With that, she turned her back and marched out of the room.

Deborah and I had an unforgettable "fame to shame" moment seven years ago. It started as one of the proudest moments of our parenting career. Like many of our memorable parenting moments, this one involved youth sports.

After learning to play tennis on Manila's slow clay courts, it took my sons some time to adjust to the speed of American hard courts. Finally, seventeen-year-old Jonathan was excelling on American hard courts. Through countless hours of disciplined training, he wasn't only winning consistently, he was beating some of the best players in the six-state United States Tennis Association (USTA) Southern Region.

Jonathan's fame moment happened at the 2007 State Tennis Championship in Chattanooga, Tennessee, when he fought and clawed his way to the finals and played one of the best matches of his life. His shame moment happened two weeks later in Little Rock, Arkansas, at the USTA Southern Regionals where he played the worst match of his life.

The shame and fame in Jonathan's case had nothing to do with winning, losing, or the quality of his game. They had everything to do with his attitude.

For several years since transferring from the Philippines to America, Jonathan had developed quite the reputation, not only for his skills and fitness, but more for his sportsmanship. Any kid who displays any level of humility and sportsmanship in junior tennis gets noticed, as there is no sport in the world with a greater concentration of bad attitudes and poor sportsmanship.

Jonathan's Moment of Fame

On the USTA junior circuit, the players call their own lines and keep their own score. Jonathan was famous for giving away point after point on close calls. He refused to argue, cheat, or even give himself the benefit of the doubt. If it was a close call, Jonathan routinely gave the point to his opponent.

At almost every high-level tournament, whether in North Carolina, Georgia, Mississippi, or Tennessee, a parent, tournament official, or coach would compliment Deborah or me about Jonathan's attitude and sportsmanship. While other competitors cheated, lost their temper, threw their rackets, argued calls, and disrespected opponents, Jonathan always seemed to lose graciously and win humbly. (Because that's how we raised him!) He always respected the USTA officials, the game, and his opponent. He never lost his temper. He took winning and losing in stride. Parents noticed. And we were proud.

That brings us to Jonathan's fame moment. After beating some good players to earn a spot in the 2007 Tennessee State finals, Jonathan lost the championship match, but he won the most prestigious sports trophy ever won by a Murrell in any sport.

For a little background, the previous year, Jonathan lost in the earlier rounds of the Tennessee State Championships to the eventual winner. The silver lining was that Jonathan was asked to be the training partner of that same kid, who lived and trained near Nashville. This opportunity was a huge privilege, since the guy was ranked as one of the top five players nationally. His mother, who also happened to be his coach, took note of Jonathan's work ethic and attitude, and asked if Jonathan would be interested in training with her son. Every competitive player in the area would have given anything to train with this kid and his mom. But she wanted Jonathan precisely because of his relentless work ethic and gracious attitude. Needless to say, in that one year, Jonathan made huge progress by training with the best.

After a year of training with them, Jonathan made it all the way to the state finals. That final match was a classic back-and-forth battle. After splitting the first two sets, Jonathan was down a break and his opponent was serving for the match. Match point was a grueling twenty-ball rally. Finally Jonathan hit the shot of the tournament, forehand down the line that landed an inch inside the baseline, right in the corner. What a gutsy shot! An all-or-nothing clear winner when he was down match point!

The few hundred parents and fans surrounding the court stood and erupted in applause, then reacted in shocked silence when they realized the other kid called it out, giving himself the game, the set, the match, and the championship.

Without reacting, complaining, arguing, or throwing his racket, Jonathan immediately jogged to the net, extended his hand to congratulate the champion, then walked to the bench to pack his rackets in his massive orange and black Hedley tennis bag.

Fifteen minutes later, during the trophy ceremony, Jonathan's opponent was awarded the championship trophy to faint applause. Then, partially because of his reputation during the whole season and partially because of his gracious reaction to being cheated on match point, Jonathan was awarded the 2007 Tennessee Tennis Sportsmanship trophy.

Over the years, our shelves have been decorated with trophies for team or individual athletic accomplishments. (We never kept the unearned participation trophies.) But this award was special because it recognized qualities that matter for life: character, heart, humility, integrity, and fair play.

When the award ceremony was over, the kid who cheated on match point was ignored, while Jonathan got surrounded by players, parents, and officials congratulating him on a great tournament. We had never been more proud.

Little did we know that just two weeks later, our pride would turn to humiliation and Jonathan's fame would turn to shame.

That's Not How We Raised You

Fast forward two weeks and cross the Mississippi River from Tennessee to Arkansas. Being the runner-up at the Tennessee State Championship qualified Jonathan for the USTA 2007 Southern Regionals in Little Rock, Arkansas. Jonathan would now compete with top players from Arkansas, Louisiana, Tennessee, Mississippi, South Carolina, and Alabama. A top sixteen finish would automatically qualify Jonathan to play in the USTA Nationals in Kalamazoo, Michigan. The USTA national champ gets an invitation to the US Open (to get clobbered in the first round by Nadal, Federer, or another pro). Jonathan knew he had no chance of winning the Nationals and playing in the US Open. His goal was simply to qualify for the Nationals and win a chance to compete with the best junior players in America.

Only hardcore tennis people will understand what happened that day in Little Rock that turned Jonathan's fame to shame, but I will try my best to explain it.

You see, Jonathan doesn't possess a killer forehand like his brother, James, who can hit a tennis ball through a brick wall. Where James wins with power, Jonathan wins with finesse, fitness, and pinpoint accuracy.

My sons grew up on Philippine clay courts. Clay court tennis requires more patience than its hard court cousin. On clay, the ball bounces higher, allowing more time to get to the ball, thus creating longer points, which require greater strategy and fitness. James, with his power game, adapted quickly to American hard court tennis with its quick points. Jonathan morphed his Asian clay court game with American hard court, resulting in a style that was built around creating long points, being in great shape, and strategic line-painting accuracy with his super-topspin forehand. Using clay court tennis strategy on hard courts got Jonathan all the way to the Southern Regionals.

Two weeks after the Tennessee finals, where he got cheated but won the Sportsmanship Award, Jonathan was competing against the top players in the South for a spot in the Nationals. If he played like he had the past couple of months, and if got a lucky draw, he had a chance to win a spot in the Nationals.

With the Southern Regionals approaching, Jonathan seemed to be peaking at the perfect time. For several months, he had been "in the zone." His serve had pop. His forehand was painting the lines. His backhand was stronger and more accurate than ever. He was in better shape than ninety-nine percent of the players he faced. He had no lingering injuries. His confidence was sky-high. He sure looked ready for this tournament.

Dude, Where's My Forehand?

But, the day before his first-round match, on the practice court, something seemed wrong. Jonathan's most potent weapon, his laser-focused forehand, did not make the trip with us from Nashville to Little Rock. The more Jonathan practiced that day, the worse his forehand performed. He was spraying balls all over the court and the stands. With his forehand missing in action, his game had gone back in time several years. His forehand had no spin, no power, and no accuracy. His confidence crashed, and his outlook for the next day was bleak.

If not for the seriousness of the setting, the pitiful collapse of his forehand would have been comical. Maybe one day we'll all laugh about his vanishing forehand at the Southern Regionals, but seven years later, it's still too soon.

This mysterious "vanishing-forehand syndrome" had afflicted him once before. Curing it had required about four hours on the court with his "stroke doctor" (Coach Jim) every day for one solid week. I'm sure Coach Jim could fix it again, but we didn't have Jim in Little Rock, and we didn't have one week. We had twenty-four hours—and me. And I'm not a tennis coach.

Mercifully, Jonathan's time on the practice court came to an end, and we went back to the hotel, hoping for an overnight miracle that would heal his ailing forehand.

The next day during the pre-match warm-up, it was immediately obvious that his miracle healing did not happen. Jonathan's formerly beautiful and once deadly forehand had regressed to his days on the beginner circuit. If something didn't happen soon, it would be ugly.

As fate would have it, it was beyond ugly.

Jonathan's forehand never showed up at the match. As a result, he not only lost his first-round match to a kid he would have easily beaten the week prior, worse, he had a complete mental meltdown. After the match was over, one by one, Jonathan's $250 rackets flew over the fence and into the parking lot. Fortunately, none of the innocent bystanders were injured. His tennis bag was already empty by the time he dropkicked it into the fence. And that was just the beginning of the breakdown. Needless to say, this was not how we raised him.

I retreated to the car, pretending not to know him and mumbling to myself about leaving him in Little Rock.

The only explanation I could offer my embarrassed wife was that as soon as we crossed the state line into Arkansas, unbeknownst to us, a UFO had captured the Jonathan Murrell with a textbook forehand and the 2007 Tennessee State Tennis Sportsmanship trophy and replaced him with this unskilled kid who was channeling John MacEnroe.

From fame to shame.

DEALING WITH DISAPPOINTMENT

What do you do when your kids act exactly opposite of how you raised them?

Here's what Deborah and I did that infamous day in Little Rock. First, we pretended we didn't know the kid on Court Sixteen who was tossing expensive rackets over the fence and dropkicking his orange and black Hedley gear bag. Secondly, we walked to our car and drove straight back to Nashville. Thirdly, we sent Jonathan a text with directions to the bus station and told him to be home by Christmas.

Not really. But I must confess, I actually considered all of the above.

Here's what we did. First, I mistakenly started with a heated, intense, and futile family discussion about attitude and being a gracious loser, not an obnoxious loser. As I've learned again and again, it's always better to delay those discussions until all parties recover their sanity and return to their right minds. This usually requires at least one hour after a horrible sporting event.

Secondly, I eventually calmed down. We had lunch. I listened to Jonathan narrate his disappointment about his delinquent forehand, his disappointment about missing the Nationals, and his sincere apology about disappointing his parents with his bad behavior.

During our parenting careers, most of us will have to deal with disappointments much more serious than an embarrassing meltdown on a tennis court, but the parenting principles are the same whether the disappointment is major or minor.

When dealing with parental disappointment, it's important to realize that we're not necessarily bad parents because our kids mess up. The father in the Parable of the Prodigal Son is honored as a shining example of how a loving father should respond to a child who messes up. We don't see him as a failure. We don't psychoanalyze and judge him because his son ate with the pigs. Also, consider the fact that God has billions of prodigals, but He's certainly not a failure as our heavenly Father.

Sometimes parents contribute to the rebellion and mistakes of their children. Sometimes they don't. It's possible and common for flawed but good-hearted parents to raise prodigals. Even a perfect parent (a.k.a. God) can end up with a rebellious child or two — or two billion. So don't be so hard on yourself or on other parents.

Rather than blaming God, myself, my wife, my church, or my children, here's what I remind myself when dealing with big or small prodigal issues and parental disappointments.

- **Be a parent, not a pastor.** In the course of their lives, my sons have had many pastors. But they have only had one mother and one father. We can outsource the pastoring, but not the parenting. If I don't fulfill the role of pastor to my sons, plenty of other pastors are ready and willing to step into that void. And many of them are better pastors than I will ever be. But if Deborah and I don't fulfill the role of parents, no one else can. If you have a prodigal who makes even the smallest step in the right direction, you might want to respond like the father in the parable who met his son with an affectionate hug, a family celebration, and undeserved generosity.

  > We can outsource the pastoring, but not the parenting.

- **Pray more, preach less.** I'm not sure, but my guess is that the father of the prodigal in the parable did a lot more praying for his son than preaching to his son. In the end, after much pain and shame, things turned out well for this famous prodigal family. If you've tried preaching to your prodigals and they're still far away, I suggest muting the sermons and replacing them with prayer.

- **Offer a listening ear, not an angry lecture.** Most return- ing prodigals know they've made some really dumb decisions. They usually don't need a finger-pointing lecture from an angry parent to confirm what reality and conscience are already screaming at them. But they do need and appreciate a patient and understanding listen- ing ear. Some of us have learned to shut our mouth to listen, but we allow our facial expressions to shout what we don't allow our tongues to say. The less the face silently shouts judgment, the better. Learn to shut up and listen, especially to prodigals and rebels.

- **Look for progress, not perfection.** As soon as the prodigal turned for home, while he was still far off, his father ran to him. He was far from home and far from perfect, but he was finally pointed in the right direction. As soon as prodigals make a turn and take a step in the right direction, rather than criticizing how far away they still are, why not try running to them with open arms and throwing a party to celebrate?

LOOK FOR PROGRESS, NOT PERFECTION

This idea of progress brings us back to the title of this chap- ter, *The Pilgrim's Progress*. John Bunyan's classic allegory of the Christian life poignantly describes the ups and downs of the Christian journey.

The main character of the story, Christian, embarks on a journey to the Celestial City. On his journey, Christian encounters various people, including Mr. Worldly Wiseman, Mr. Legality, Madam Bubble, The Interpreter, The Lion,

Apollyon, Beelzebub, Obstinate, Evangelist, Little Faith, Shame, Envy, Mercy, and Mr. Great-Heart.

Some of these people help Christian on his journey—others not so much.

Christian visits some interesting places on his journey to the Celestial City, including the City of Destruction, Delectable Mountains, Doubting Castle, Enchanting Grounds, Pillar of Salt, and the Valley of Humiliation. But the most important and life-changing site along the way had to be the Cross and Sepulchre, where Christian's burdens are finally lifted off his weary shoulders.

> As parents, we should see and celebrate progress, rather than expect and demand perfection.

Bunyan used two well-chosen words in his title that every parent should embrace, whether they're raising prodigals or angels.

- **Pilgrim.** Bunyan pictures Christians as pilgrims. A pilgrim is a person on a journey, usually a very important spiritual journey. Bunyan rightly sees the Christian life as a pilgrimage, a direction, a lifelong journey, rather than a set of beliefs or religious traditions. Likewise, parenting is a journey, a very important spiritual journey. Like most journeys, the parenting journey will have ups and downs, valleys and hills. Our kids will meet many colorful characters along the way. It helps me to see kids as pilgrims and to see parenting as a journey.

- **Progress.** If the Christian life is a journey, then the goal is progress. As parents, we should see and celebrate progress, rather than expect and demand perfection. Only one person was ever perfect, and He was Jesus. The rest of us are not even close. If you're dealing with a prodigal, look for and celebrate progress in the right direction rather than obsessing over the lack of perfection.

HOW TO FORGIVE AND FORGET

We will end this chapter with a story about celebrating progress, not perfection.

It was Saturday night and James, my eight-year-old, was completing his daily ritual of writing in his journal before bedtime. His brothers were asleep, so I tiptoed into the room and whispered: "Time to turn that light off and go to bed; it's late."

"Okay. I'm almost finished."

"What are you writing about, anyway?"

"The game!" He answered as if nothing else could possibly be worth writing about on that particular Saturday, and he couldn't understand why anyone would even ask. Of course! He was writing about the game. I should have known that.

Here's what he wrote about the game.

> October 27, 1996. Today, we had our first baseball game. Our team is the Mariners. I got a home run. We won the game thirteen to zero. The other team was the Mets. I played shortstop.

James played baseball. His team won. He hit a home run. That's about all that really matters to an eight-year-old Little Leaguer.

He hit his home run the third time he batted. He was so proud of his big hit that he conveniently forgot about the other two times he batted. It's amazing how selective memory develops at such an early age.

Since James decided to forget his first two times to bat, I decided not to remind him that he struck out both times. I told him that I was really proud of him. I kissed him on the forehead, turned off his light, and tiptoed out of the room.

As I lay in bed that night, I thought about how glad I am to serve a God who records my home runs and "forgets" my strikeouts. I'm so thankful He doesn't constantly remind me of all my dumb decisions, bad attitudes, and past sins.

As parents, I'm not at all suggesting that we should live in unreality and pretend we never do anything wrong, or that as parents, we should ignore the rebellion and bad behavior of our children. Spiritually speaking, we can only forget our strikeouts after we repent and receive God's forgiveness. Our conscience exists to make sure we never forget until we experience sincere confession and real repentance.

> I silently prayed that I would be the kind of parent who was a living example of a father who forgives and forgets.

That night in bed, I silently prayed that I would be the kind of parent who was a living example of a father who forgives and forgets. I know my young sons see God through the lens of my example. That's a scary thought.

Once we face and confess our sins, our God chooses to forgive and purify us from all unrighteousness (1 John 1:9). He chooses to remove our sins as far as the east is from the west (Psalm 103:12). He chooses to hurl all our iniquities into the depths of the sea (Micah 7:19). Because of the blood of Jesus, we don't have to live in sin, defeat, guilt, and condemnation any longer. In short, God forgives and forgets.

I love my sons when they hit home runs and when they strike out. Of course, they're much happier when they hit home runs. Striking out is never much fun. The spiritual parallel is obvious. God loves us when we stay on the straight and narrow path to the Celestial City, and when we detour to the City of Destruction, Delectable Mountains, Doubting Castle, and the Pillar of Salt. When we hit home runs and when we strike out. His love is constant, no matter how poorly we perform. Of course, life is much more fun for us when we're hitting home runs than when we're striking out.

DISCUSSION QUESTIONS

1. How did your parents deal with you when you rebelled against and disappointed them? Was it helpful or hurtful?

2. From your experience, what is the most challenging aspect of parenting a prodigal child?

3. Practically speaking, how can you be more like the father in the Parable of the Prodigal Son when your children rebel?

HOME

9

WHERE THE WILD THINGS ARE
Discipleship Starts at Home

And Max, the king of all wild things, was lonely and wanted to be where someone loved him best of all.
Maurice Sendak, *Where the Wild Things Are*

"Go into all the world and preach the gospel to every creature."
Mark 16:15 (NKJV)

And they said, "Believe in the Lord Jesus, and you will be saved, you and your household."
Acts 16:31

In the famous children's book by Maurice Sendak, *Where the Wild Things Are*, a young boy named Max is sent to his bedroom without dinner because of his disruptive behavior. One of my favorite lines is when he threatens his mom by saying, "I'll eat you up!" After storming off to his room, Max — with his wild imagination — turns his room into a jungle full of "wild things." But after exploring his exciting imaginary world by boat and partying with the wild animals, Max realizes that he misses home. He had become the king of the wild things, but it turns out what he really wanted was to be back home with his parents. So he sails back to reality (a.k.a. his bedroom), and finds a hot dinner waiting for him.

Sendak's imaginative children's story reminds me of two truths about parenting.

First, home is a special place. For Max, home was not only a *place* where his *family* lived, it was a place "where someone loved him best of all." What a beautiful description of home and family. Second, this story reminds me that one of the most exciting, difficult, and exotic mission fields is our own home. Whether you have two kids or ten, boys or girls, toddlers or teenagers — you can probably identify with Max's parents whose own home turned out to be where the wild things are.

> Whether you feel called to serve Muslims in Afghanistan, Buddhists in Cambodia, or your neighbors and coworkers right where you are in Nashville, your most important missionary call is to make disciples in your own home.

What is your home like? Is it a place where your children feel unconditional love — even when they act like wild things? Do you see your home as a mission field, a place where you're called to make disciples — just as valid as a traditional mission field in an Amazon jungle or an African savannah?

In the last section (chapters four through eight), we looked at the importance of the heart. In this section (chapters nine and ten), we'll explore the importance of the home — the place where love, correction, discipleship, and leadership development should happen.

WIKICHURCH AT HOME

As a cross-cultural missionary and a leader in a global church planting movement, I love thinking about new mission fields. One of my greatest joys is meeting with young church planters and campus missionaries and hearing them talk about where God has called them to take the gospel.

Earlier today I was on my monthly conference call with Every Nation regional directors in Africa, Asia, Europe, Latin America, Middle East, and North America. On that call, Dr. Jun Escosar, our Asia regional director, reported that forty-four recent graduates of our Every Nation School of World Missions are now in the process of relocating to twenty-one nations. Those target nations include Afghanistan, Azerbaijan, Cambodia, Fiji, Jordan, Kazakhstan, Mongolia, Nepal, Oman, and others.

Yet as exciting, challenging, and significant as those new mission fields are, the most important mission field any of us will ever be on is in our home.

Whether you feel called to serve Muslims in Afghanistan, Buddhists in Cambodia, or your neighbors and coworkers right where you are in Nashville, your most important missionary call is to make disciples in your own home.

When Jesus commanded us to "Go therefore and make disciples of all nations" (Matthew 28:19), He never intended for us to leave our family out of the mission. He never wanted us to choose family or mission. He called us to both.

Consider the book of Acts. Over and over again, when people became disciples, it was rarely an individual decision — it usually involved the whole family.

- When Peter preached in Cornelius's home (Acts 10), the entire household responded to the message. Everyone was baptized in the Holy Spirit and water.

- When Paul and Silas preached to the Philippian jailer (Acts 16) and he asked them, "Sirs, what must I do to be saved?" They responded, "Believe in the Lord Jesus, and you will be saved, you and *your household*." So "he *and all his family*" were baptized that day.

- When Paul ministered in Corinth (Acts 18:8), we learn that Crispus, the leader of the synagogue, "believed in the Lord, together with his entire household."

- Finally, in his letter to the church in Corinth, Paul talks about baptizing "the household of Stephanas" (1 Corinthians 1:16).

God's mission is not merely about redeeming individuals — His desire is to redeem and transform entire families.

With these examples, I'm not trying to suggest that every member of every family always comes to Jesus at the same time and pace. Sometimes entire families become followers of Jesus in rapid succession, and sometimes, families are reached gradually, one member at a time over a long period of time. Either way, what we learn from these examples is that God's mission is not merely about redeeming individuals — His desire is to redeem and transform entire families.

Salvation is never just about you. It's about you and your household.

In ancient Near Eastern cultures, the idea that an individual's conversion would lead to an entire family's conversion was not revolutionary. However, in highly individualistic Westernized cultures, discipleship is often seen as a solely individual pursuit. Though we can appreciate the modern ideal of freedom of conscience, we should not take this so far as to assume that discipleship can or should be divorced from the context of family.

I would go so far as to argue that discipleship and family are meant to go together. Why? Because discipleship starts at home.

In my book, *WikiChurch*, I wrote at length about the "Four Es" that comprise our discipleship process at Victory Manila, my home church in the Philippines. The Four Es are a simple way to remember the key components in the discipleship journey. Here they are:

- *Engage* culture and community (with the goal of preaching the gospel)
- *Establish* biblical foundations
- *Equip* believers to minister
- *Empower* disciples to make disciples

For the last three decades, I've preached and practiced this simple discipleship process countless times in the Philippines and all over the world. I've also preached and practiced these same Four Es in my home.

What does it look like to apply the Four Es in the home? How do we *engage* our children with the gospel? How do we *establish* biblical foundations? How do we *equip* our kids to minister to their friends and classmates? And how do we *empower* our kids to make disciples?

ENGAGE: OUR FUNNIEST HOME VIDEOS

Discipleship—whether at church or at home—begins with intentional engagement. In the same way that we can't make disciples without engaging the lost, we can't be good parents without engaging our children. This may seem like a strange concept. Why would we need to intentionally engage our children if we raised them in our own home? Wouldn't we know them quite well by default?

Yes and no.

While you probably know your own children better than most people do, children change and develop at such a fast rate while they're in your home, the task of knowing them and engaging them never stops.

For example, imagine that you were, for some reason, separated from your family for ten years. Even if you knew your six-year-old daughter really well before you were separated, by the time you returned ten years later, your now sixteen-year-old daughter would practically be a new person. Her interests, her hobbies, her personality, her perspective on life—all of it would have changed. Your challenge as a parent would be to engage and know your sixteen-year-old daughter, allowing the memories of the six-year old version to become just that—memories.

Many parents recognize the importance of engaging and relationally connecting with their children. But they often don't know how — especially when their children hit the teen years. Many fantastic parenting books deal with this specific issue, but I'll offer a simple question that has helped me stay engaged and connected with my sons over the years.

What's Your Hobby?

Some parents have hobbies. And some claim to be too busy for hobbies. Some parents play a sport. Some play an instrument. Some read. Some watch (way too much) TV. Some travel. When I first moved to the Philippines, I used to play basketball in our neighborhood park. A few years later, I started mountain biking with men in my church. But as my sons moved beyond the toddler stage, my hobbies changed.

When William, James, and Jonathan were in elementary school, my hobby was coaching baseball. I began as a novice assistant coach on my oldest son's T-ball team when he was six. By the time my second son started baseball, I was promoted to head coach. This meant that I was in charge of midweek practices and weekend games. I was responsible not only to manage a bunch of six- to nine-year-olds on the field but also their rowdy parents in the stands. As my kids got more into baseball, I continued my hobby/responsibility as head coach (sometimes of multiple teams). Eventually, I was involved with three different teams in three different age-group leagues. My Saturdays were spent racing from one game to the next to the next. Also, I served on the Board of Directors for the International Little League Association of Manila for a decade.

In short, from 1992 to 2002, baseball was my hobby. It wasn't because I enjoyed coaching baseball more than mountain biking. It was because William, James, and Jonathan enjoyed baseball more than mountain biking. Baseball was their hobby, so it became mine.

I didn't sign them up for baseball so that I could have somewhere to drop my sons off for a few hours twice a week. I signed them up for baseball so that we could have a common point of interest for the next ten years of their lives. I signed them up to create memories together. And we created some really great memories!

It's important to note that my baseball hobby wasn't just about my sons and me. Deborah also fully bought in. She never missed a game. To this day, some of our favorite family videos are ones that Deborah took during baseball games. They're our favorites not because the games were particularly exciting, but because of her enthusiastic commentary and her less-than-focused camera work. Remember, these were the pre-cell phone, pre-digital days of huge video cameras. Since I was on the field coaching, Deborah was in the stands as our designated family videographer.

Imagine you're now watching a grainy Murrell home video from twenty years ago. Six-year-old James is at bat. I'm coaching first base, barking instructions like we're in the World Series. Jonathan is in the bleachers playing with his G.I. Joes. Deborah is drinking her iced tea (with extra ice) when suddenly James smashes the ball into the outfield and sprints towards first base. Iced tea in one hand, Deborah aims the camera with the other.

> James got a hit! Run James. RUN! Faster. FASTER! Keep running to second . . . Jonathan, stop climbing on those bleachers . . . Keep running James . . . Jonathan, I said, DO NOT climb the bleachers . . . Run James RUN! Jonathan . . .

What's more, any time the game had real action—when one of our sons got a hit or made a defensive play—we have clear audio, but the video is almost never captured on camera because Deborah would usually drop the camera and cheer. Many of our sons' greatest baseball moments are accompanied with extensive footage of feet and bleachers with the sound of Deborah cheering.

The Family that Plays Together Stays Together

In their early teen years, my sons shifted away from baseball and started playing competitive tennis. Since I had played baseball growing up, it was easy for me to connect with my sons over baseball and teach them the game. But tennis was totally new for me. Needless to say, I didn't become their tennis coach. But Deborah and I did become avid tennis parents. We learned the rules, we spoke the jargon, we bought the clothes and expensive rackets, and we traveled to tournaments. Prior to 2003, Deborah and I didn't care about tennis. But after our sons got into it, we became tennis fanatics.

Tennis was our new family hobby. Why? Not because we loved tennis, but because our sons loved tennis—and we loved them.

In many ways, tennis is a very inconvenient and expensive hobby. I can't tell you how many hours we spent melting in the summer sun at Rizal Racket Club in Manila, or later, Centennial Sportsplex in Nashville. I can't remember how many days we spent on the road driving to tennis tournaments. I've lost track of how many dollars we spent on tennis gear, tournament fees, coaching clinics, hotel rooms, and tennis camps.

> Because Deborah and I were at almost every game and many practices, we were in a place to recognize and leverage discipleship opportunities that helped shape our sons' hearts.

Eventually William, James, and Jonathan all received athletic scholarships to play college tennis in America, but considering how much money we spent on tennis, I'm still not convinced it was a sound financial investment. Honestly, it doesn't matter because it was never about the scholarships.

I'm grateful that our sons got athletic scholarships, but the real reason Deborah and I got into tennis — the real reason we invested our time and money — was because we wanted to engage our sons. It was about celebrating their success and empowering their dreams. It was about connecting with them in their world.

I can't tell you how many discipleship moments spontaneously happened on the way home from a tennis match or baseball game. These moments usually occurred after a heartbreaking loss or an on-court meltdown. Because my sons were (and still are) highly competitive and heavily invested in their sports, wins and especially losses opened up their souls in ways that they never opened in any other context. And because Deborah and I were at almost every game and many practices, we were in a place to recognize and leverage discipleship opportunities that helped shape our sons' hearts. We were there to listen to their disappointments and help them work through anger issues without breaking expensive tennis rackets. Being at their sporting events enabled us to teach them how to lose graciously and how to win humbly.

Maybe your children aren't into sports. You'll still need to figure out how to engage their world and their interests. Learn to love what they love. Pursue what they pursue. Make their hobbies your hobbies. If you do, you'll find that opportunities to share the gospel and shape their character will constantly present themselves. More importantly, you'll demonstrate to them that their heavenly Father is interested in the small details of their lives.

ESTABLISH: THE FAMILY THAT PRAYS TOGETHER . . .

If engaging our children is about recognizing and maximizing spontaneous lifestyle discipleship moments, then establishing spiritual foundations is about intentionally planned discipleship moments. When I say planned, I don't mean rigid or formulaic, but I do mean regular and consistent — and planned.

Before we discuss some practical ways to establish biblical foundations at home, it might be helpful to look at the endgame. Jesus talked about two houses that were hit by strong storms. The house with the strong foundation endured the storm. The house that had weak foundations collapsed. (See Matthew 7:24–27.)

As parents, our job is not to make sure our children never experience the storms of life. Our job is to establish deep biblical foundations so our kids will stand strong when the inevitable storms of life hit the hardest.

Here are three essential foundations that must be established if our children are to thrive during stormy seasons.

- **Established in the Word.** It's our responsibility as parents to teach the Bible to our children. It's great if they learn something at church. But that's only once a week. It's great if they go to a Christian school and take Bible classes. But from the ages of zero to eighteen, no one is more responsible for a child's biblical education than parents. Do your children know the basic outline of the biblical story? Do they find the Bible and its stories exciting and fascinating? Do they know how the story of Jesus fits into the larger narrative of redemption? Do they know the difference between Noah and Moses?

> As parents, our job is not to make sure our children never experience the storms of life. Our job is to establish deep biblical foundations so our kids will stand strong when the inevitable storms of life hit the hardest.

- **Established in the faith.** More than just teaching Bible stories, our goal as parents is to impart to our children a basic understanding of the gospel and theology. To establish our children in the faith means we make sure they understand salvation, water baptism, and the baptism of the Holy Spirit. It's never too early to start teaching children theology — for theology is simply the study of God. Sure, sometimes theology can be complex. How do you explain the virgin birth to a six-year-old? How do you explain the Trinity to a twelve-year-old who is certain that one plus one plus one equals three, not one? And how do you talk about sin and judgment with a sixteen-year-old who finds the idea of hell unfair? These conversations are all complicated, but they're all worth having. Are you creating space to have these and other faith conversations?

> It's our responsibility as parents to teach the Bible to our children.

- **Established in church community.** In an age where many millennials are leaving church, it's important that we instill in our children a deep love for church community. If we raise children who know the Bible well and understand the gospel deeply but don't think that church community matters, then we have a recipe for disaster. Why? Because God never intended for us to be autonomous, individualistic Christians. He made us to connect with others, and He gave us a mission that can only be completed together. Do your children love your church? Maybe a more important question is, do you love your local church?

If engaging our children is about entering their world, then establishing biblical foundations is about introducing them to new worlds — the world of the Bible. The world of the Kingdom of God. And the world of church history.

Establishing children in God's Word involves teaching them the Bible and, more importantly, teaching them to love the Bible — and eventually to read it on their own. Consistent family devotions that involve reading and retelling Bible stories is crucial. Be creative. Buy a children's Bible with good pictures when your children are young. Watch *The Bible* TV series with your children. Create regular opportunities for Bible reading and discussion in your home. And if your children aren't enjoying family devotions, then go back to the drawing board and find new ways to make the time more engaging. Whatever you do, do something. Make spiritual development at home a priority.

Beyond Family Devotions

Even more important than group family devotions is cultivating in children the discipline of personal Bible study and prayer. This is often difficult to figure out as children learn to read at different ages and some children enjoy reading more than others. When they were younger, Deborah and I bought Bibles for our sons that corresponded with their reading levels and age group. You can find Kids Study Bibles, Pre-teen Study Bibles, Teen Study Bibles, College Study Bibles — more Bibles than you can possibly imagine. Daily devotional guides — with a short Scripture, devotional passage, and application section — are another helpful tool. Sometimes my sons enjoyed the daily devotional books — other times they never opened them.

Every child is different, but the goal is the same. You want your children to develop a hunger for God's Word. You want them to develop spiritual disciplines. You want them to engage their mind with the Scriptures. You want them to see the biblical narrative of redemption as the greatest and most exciting story ever told.

This will only happen if we as parents make this a priority in our families — and in our own lives. Do you have a passion for the Word? Do your children see you reading the Bible and praying every day? Do they know that it matters to you?

Establishing children in the faith is all about showing children how the stories and teachings in the Bible relate to us today. This begins with a basic understanding of the gospel, but it doesn't stop there. Our goal in teaching our children the Word and the gospel is that it will transform the way they think, act, feel, and live. In other words, we don't just want our children to understand the world of Jesus in the gospels. We want our children to understand the world — or Kingdom — that Jesus began and still rules today. The Kingdom of God operates differently than the temporal world. Do our children understand how and why? Or do they see Christianity as merely a moral framework?

Obviously, establishing our children in the faith is not easy. In fact, it can't be done without the work of the Holy Spirit in their hearts. But God uses parents to teach faith to children and explain how the Bible applies to our lives today. God uses parents to discuss with children the implications of the death and resurrection of Jesus, and to teach them the mind-blowing significance of the Incarnation. Parents are supposed to challenge their children to live and think like citizens of the Kingdom of God, and to demonstrate to them what it looks like to live a Spirit-empowered life.

The Power of Church History

One of the best ways to show them what real Spirit-empowered Christianity looks like is to introduce them to the world of church history. There are many good ways to do this (and some really boring ways to do this), but in our family, Deborah and I read missionary biographies to our children. Lots of them — William Carey, Adoniram Judson, Nicolaus Zinzendorf, John Wesley, David Livingstone, Hudson Taylor, Eric Liddell. To this day, my sons probably know more about the leaders of the Modern Mission Movement than they know about the leaders of the American Revolution.

I wouldn't have it any other way.

> When we prayed together for our missionary friends, we weren't only teaching our children to pray for the nations — we were also teaching them to value church community.

They eventually learned some American and world history at school, but our goal was to teach them church history — to tell them exciting stories about real people who responded sacrificially to God's mission and how God worked through them for His glory and for the transformation of nations. I would strongly encourage you to read engaging biographies of great Christians — past and present — to your children. Show them that they are connected to a story and to a people who have a long and exciting history.

Show them that they too can join in God's mission by partnering with His people today. Not only did Deborah and I tell our children missionary stories from the past; we told them stories about real missionaries from our churches.

And we prayed with our kids for our missionaries. We didn't sugarcoat it. Even as young boys, they knew that we were often praying for life and death mission field situations involving real people and good friends in Bangladesh, China, Myanmar, Vietnam, Russia, and other nations. These were missionaries who had spoken in our church and slept in our home, and we were now praying for them as a family. When we prayed together for our missionary friends, we weren't only teaching our children to pray for the nations — we were also teaching them to value church community.

EQUIP: THE MYTH OF MATURITY

In *WikiChurch*, I talk about the "Myth of Maturity" — the idea that only "spiritually mature" Christians can make disciples. While I'm all for veteran Christians being involved in discipleship, I want to make sure that new and inexperienced Christians aren't then excluded from making disciples because "maturity" is an absolute criteria. What's more, whether church leaders say it explicitly or we say it to ourselves internally, we will always find ways to fall short of the elusive state of Christian maturity. What we learn from the experiences of Jesus' disciples, who were far from mature when they started, is that Christians can't grow in maturity unless they start making disciples.

What does this mean for the church? It means that no disciple is too young and inexperienced to begin making disciples. All they need is to be equipped.

So what does this mean for the family? If you buy into the idea that Christians—no matter how new and inexperienced—ought to be involved in making disciples, then what does this mean for your eight-year-old? It means that your children are never too young to be equipped to make disciples.

Who said there was an age limit on making disciples? People often don't believe me when I say this, but at Victory in Manila, we have nine- to fourteen-year-olds leading small groups with their classmates. We've created a kids' version of the *ONE 2 ONE* discipleship book as well as other small group materials specifically geared towards that age group. Obviously, these kids show a lot of maturity and spiritual passion, but nearly every single one of them has parents who model a lifestyle of discipleship and have equipped them to make disciples.

Discipleship at McDonald's

My oldest son, William, started going to his first discipleship group when he was in elementary school. It was led by our kids' pastor, Rommel. After a few months, their group of eight turned into dozens of nine- to twelve-year-olds. Perhaps part of the secret was that they met in the McDonald's in the mall. As more kids kept coming, Rommel (who was in his twenties) brought in some thirteen- and fourteen-year-olds to help disciple the influx of kids. So Rommel would lead a group at one table, Danny (thirteen) would lead a group at another table, and Deon (thirteen) would lead a group at the next table.

As they continued to grow, William, who was about eleven, was asked to help lead one of the groups. He wasn't given full responsibility overnight, but he was assigned small tasks at first. For example, one week Rommel asked him to select and ask the opening question. The next week, he was responsible for teaching one of the three points. I'll never forget William preparing for this one point. He had multiple illustrations, personal stories, a dozen Bible verses, and lots of subpoints—all for three minutes of airtime.

Eventually, Rommel moved away to be a missionary in Latvia, but William had gotten the bug. He wanted to make disciples. And he had been equipped as an eleven-year-old.

When he was thirteen, he started a discipleship group with his classmates at school during lunch—using the same small group material, and often the exact same notes he had used in Rommel's group a few years earlier. This group continued in different shapes and forms throughout William's time in middle school and high school. Many of William's classmates started coming to church with him and some even began discipleship groups of their own.

Though I still give much of the credit for William's passion for discipleship to his early young adult small group leaders—Rommel, Rico, and Paolo—Deborah and I were also involved in encouraging and equipping William to make disciples. How?

First, he saw us modeling a discipleship lifestyle. William probably can't remember a time in his life when we weren't leading discipleship groups. Deborah usually led small groups in our home, and I usually had them at coffee shops. But our sons always knew that small group discipleship was a priority—not because we were pastors but because we were Christians.

Second, from a young age, we equipped our sons to pray — not only for the nations but also for their unsaved friends and neighbors. Prayer is the fuel for discipleship. Do you pray with your kids? Do you pray with them for their unsaved friends, classmates, and teammates? Do they see you prioritizing discipleship?

Empower: How to Not Lose Your Faith In College

One of the great fears of Christian parents is that their children will lose their faith when they get to college. Whether it's prompted by intellectual challenges, new peers and influences, or an inability to connect with church community, many people who grow up in Christian homes do experience faith struggles in college. As a result, dozens of books have been written for parents to help prevent this trend from affecting their family.

> Do you pray with your kids? Do you pray with them for their unsaved friends, classmates, and teammates?

While many of the books give some great advice, I think that the entire approach is wrong.

Imagine a ship-building manual entitled *How to Make a Ship that Doesn't Sink*. I'm glad that people make ships that don't sink, but that's kind of a low bar. Ships are meant to do more than just not sink. They are meant to go somewhere. In the same way, I hope your kids don't lose their faith in college. But there's a lot more to it than that. Our goal as parents is not that our kids would merely stay afloat while in college. Our goal is that they would be equipped and empowered to go somewhere and do something that honors God and changes the world.

In fact, the best way to make sure that your kids don't lose their faith in college is to equip and empower them as disciple-makers. The goal should be loftier than avoiding "bad influences." The goal should be to influence their classmates. The goal is not to survive intellectual challenges; the goal is to think critically and see how the Word applies to every area of life — even academia. The goal is not to find an insulated community of Christians on campus and hang out with them only — the goal is to join other Christians in engaging the campus with the gospel.

So how do we empower our children to make disciples?

Engaging our kids is about entering their world. Establishing them in the faith is about introducing them to new worlds. Equipping them to minister is about teaching them to pray and creating small opportunities for them to minister. And empowering our kids is about encouraging them to take steps of faith and trusting them and the Holy Spirit in them to succeed.

Empowering involves one of the most difficult acts as a parent — letting go of control.

William's First Attempt at Preaching
When William was a senior in high school, he came home one day with a puzzled yet excited look on his face. He explained to Deborah and me that one of his friends on the student council had asked him if he would be willing to speak at the upcoming school banquet. (This particular Christian school didn't believe in dances; they believed in banquets.) William was a little confused, but his friend explained that

the student council wanted to have a spiritual component to the banquet and his name came up as a speaker.

"Why me?" William asked. Then Stephen, his friend who was not only a student council member but was also in William's discipleship group, explained, "We love the stuff you talk about at discipleship group at lunch, so we thought you could say something similar at the banquet."

As William explained this to us, he was interested but not sure if he wanted to do it. He didn't have much experience speaking in public. And while he was involved in the youth group at church, his involvement was through small group discipleship and playing drums or keys on the worship team. Even though his dad was a preacher, he had never preached. He didn't know what to say to a group of his peers at a banquet. And he didn't know if he would be able to pull it off, even if he did have something to say.

Deborah and I encouraged William not to think too much about all of the obstacles, but rather to pray about the opportunity and see if the Holy Spirit put anything on his heart to talk about.

A few days later, William told us that he had something he wanted to say. So he told Stephen that he was in, and he began preparing. As a father and someone who preaches for a living, I so badly wanted to give William my best sermon and (over) coach him as he prepared. But I decided to stay back and let William prepare what he felt the Holy Spirit was leading him to talk about. He was seventeen. He had been in our home for nearly two decades.

We had been engaging his world for seventeen years. We had been establishing biblical foundations for seventeen years.

We had been equipping him to minister for seventeen years. Now it was time to empower him.

A few days before the big banquet, William asked me to look over his notes and listen to his ten-minute talk. His topic was about cultivating spiritual passion. His main point was that every battle in the Christian life comes down to passion. If we fight the battle for spiritual passion, then we will win the battle for sexual purity. But if we don't actively cultivate a passion for Jesus and His Kingdom, then we will constantly struggle in the battle for purity. In other words, our goal as young people is not merely to "stay pure," our goal is to develop a passion for Jesus and His Kingdom.

Since it was a high school banquet, Deborah and I were not allowed to attend. And, since those were the days before every phone had a video camera, we don't have footage of William's talk. In short, we never saw it. And we have no idea how it went besides William's modest comment that it went "fine," even though he forgot a few parts.

William's Second Attempt at Preaching
The only indication that things went better than "fine" was that William was asked by the school chaplain (who happened to be an official chaperone at the banquet) if he would be willing to give a similar talk to the entire high school at their weekly chapel. When William told us about the opportunity, he had a similar mixture of excitement and terror. As long as William had been at his school, students had never been the main speaker in chapel. How would his classmates respond to him being the chapel speaker? How would he come up with something new to talk about—this time for fifteen to twenty minutes?

Deborah and I encouraged him to pray about it and see if the Holy Spirit put anything on his heart to talk about. Turns out, He did.

A few weeks later, William spoke at chapel to the entire high school about actively participating in God's mission. His main point was that in the Kingdom of God, there are no non-combatants. Everyone has a role. Everyone is called to make disciples. Again, Deborah and I didn't get to attend chapel (William wouldn't let us), but we did get to watch the video.

Shortly before William graduated, a faculty advisor for the incoming student council asked William — who was taking a gap year to work on his tennis before college — if he would be willing to speak at the spiritual life retreat at the beginning of the next school year. Every year at William's school, in the first month of the new school year, all of the highschoolers participated in a weekend retreat. Usually, the student council invited an outside speaker to lead the retreat, but this time, everyone wanted William to speak.

William's Third Attempt at Preaching
While he had a whopping two public-speaking appearances under his belt, this was different. Deborah and I were a bit shocked when he explained what this opportunity entailed. Not only was he speaking at the retreat — he was the only speaker. Not only was he responsible to speak five times over the weekend, he was responsible to choose the topics and theme of the retreat. William felt honored that he was asked but totally overwhelmed by the opportunity. It was one thing to prepare hours and hours for a twenty-minute chapel talk, but what about being the main retreat speaker and speaking five times in a weekend?

Was our eighteen-year-old ready for this?

Deborah and I encouraged him to pray about it and see if the Holy Spirit put anything on his heart to talk about.

We sensed that God wanted to use him to challenge and influence his peers. He had been making disciples on that campus since he was thirteen. Nothing had really changed. He had just been presented with a bigger platform. And it wasn't a coincidence that William got these opportunities. Though he was never involved in the student council, for several years, it was filled with his friends—who also happened to be members of his discipleship group. Being asked to speak at the spiritual life retreat wasn't any different. Both the outgoing and the incoming student council presidents were in his discipleship group and he suspected they had something to do with making him the speaker at the spiritual life retreat.

After graduation, William spent the summer playing and coaching tennis—and preparing to speak at the retreat. Again, I helped him when he asked for help. But I mostly encouraged him to be bold and listen to the Holy Spirit. That fall, William spoke at the retreat—all five sessions—and according to all accounts, it went well. Again, Deborah and I were barred from attending.

Many people who heard William speak assumed that he would become a pastor like his dad. But we all knew that William's steps of faith had less to do with a call to vocational ministry and more to do with a desire to make disciples. He never wanted to speak in public. All he wanted to do was make disciples on his campus.

Today, ten years later, William is not a pastor; he's a historian. His goal is to teach, write, and become a college professor. While he's certainly a gifted public speaker, William has preached or spoken in public only a handful of times. But he never stopped making disciples — whether in college in Nashville or in graduate school in England.

DISCIPLESHIP STARTS AT HOME

I've said it countless times, and I will say it again, discipleship starts at home. My most important disciples are my sons. Deborah and I endeavored to teach them to be a disciple and how to make disciples. We did this by *engaging* their world, *establishing* biblical foundations, *equipping* them to do ministry, and *empowering* them to make disciples.

Have my sons been perfect? Absolutely not, but neither were Peter, James, or John. It was direction, not perfection, that qualified the early disciples to be used by God. And it's progress, not perfection, that qualifies us to make disciples today. As long as our kids are making progress and moving in the right direction, they can help others in their discipleship journey.

I hope you're involved in making disciples in small groups in your local church. Along with that, I hope you're making disciples at home, *where the wild things are,* and where "someone loves us best of all."

DISCUSSION QUESTIONS

1. What are some practical ways you can engage your children in this season of their lives?

2. What are you doing as a parent to establish spiritual foundations in your children? What has worked for your family? What hasn't?

3. Do you and your spouse have a lifestyle of discipleship that would communicate to your kids the importance of being and making disciples?

10

GREAT EXPECTATIONS
Leadership Development Starts at Home

I have been bent and broken, but—I hope—into a better shape.

Charles Dickens, *Great Expectations*

No varnish can hide the grain of the wood; and the more varnish you put on, the more the grain will express itself.

Charles Dickens, *Great Expectations*

Praise the Lord! Blessed is the man who fears the Lord, who greatly delights in his commandments! His offspring will be mighty in the land . . .

Psalm 112:1,2

I f you grew up in the American school system, odds are that you were forced to read the famous Charles Dickens novel, *Great Expectations*, at some point in your education. As usual, I opted to read the CliffNotes.

In this classic novel, Dickens tells the story of a poor orphan named Pip, who lives with his mean-spirited older sister and her kind husband, Joe. As a boy, Pip looks up to Joe as a father figure, and even becomes his apprentice as a black-smith. However, as a young man, Pip finds out that he has an anonymous benefactor who has provided an education for him in London so he can become a gentleman.

While in London, Pip receives an education and new friends and is transformed into an English gentleman. Yet, in spite of his new social standing and the new opportunities, Pip is haunted by a nagging question: "Is my benefactor to be made known to me today?"

Why does Pip so badly want to know who his benefactor is?

On the surface, Pip is simply curious. He wants to know who he has to thank for his change in fortunes. But on a deeper level, Pip, as an orphan, is anxious. He wants to know who's really looking out for him. Who's invested in his future?

As a child, the answer was simple — Joe the blacksmith was the only person invested in Pip and his future. After the anonymous benefactor enters the story and Pip moves to London, he immediately finds new friends and mentors, but it's difficult to tell who genuinely cares about him and who's only interested in his money.

> Parents are supposed to be the most invested in their children's future. They should have the greatest expectations for their children.

I won't spoil the plot, but Pip eventually does find out who is benefactor is — and that's when the story gets really interesting . . .

But what does Pip's burning question have to do with parenting?

LEADERSHIP DEVELOPMENT STARTS AT HOME

In many ways, every child — orphan or not — confronts the same questions that haunt Pip throughout the story: "Who is my benefactor? Who's invested in my future? Who has great expectations for my life? And who's willing to make the financial and relational sacrifices to help me realize those expectations?"

The obvious answer is that parents are supposed to be the most invested in their children's future. They should have the greatest expectations for their children. And they're the ones who are supposed to make the financial and relational sacrifices to help their children reach their potential.

Sometimes they do. Sometimes they don't.

How can we as parents — whether we're rich or poor, educated or uneducated — invest in our children's future and help them realize the great expectations that God has for their lives?

To me, the answer to that question is simple: train them to be leaders.

Leadership training may seem like a strange concept to add to a parenting book. Isn't that something that happens when our children move off to college or get their first job? Isn't that something they can learn from reading a John Maxwell book or going to a conference?

What does parenting have to do with leadership training?

Everything!

Think about it, our children are in our homes for about eighteen years before they leave for college. Sure, they'll grow and change a lot while they're in college and when they get their first job. But the discipleship and leadership foundations that we build in our children during those first eighteen years will drastically make an impact on how they grow and mature as leaders during their four years in college and their first few years out of college.

In other words, any positive growth our children have as leaders in their twenties will be built on the foundation we built while they were in their teens — and even younger.

It doesn't mean that people with less-than-perfect parents can't become great leaders. It just means that, like Pip, they will have to find benefactors and mentors elsewhere.

So how do we train our children to be leaders?

At Victory in Manila, we have a leadership training process called iLead. Like the Four Es of our discipleship process, we have Four Is for leadership development: *Identification*, *Instruction*, *Impartation*, and *Internship*. This is how we develop all leaders — from administrative staff to worship leaders, campus missionaries to church planters.

What does it look like if we apply this same leadership development process to our children at home?

Identifying God-Given Strengths in Our Children

The start of our leadership training process at church is identification—helping potential leaders identify their strengths, gifts, talents, and calling.

Who better to initiate this process of discovery than parents?

As parents, we spend nearly two decades watching our children grow in our homes. We're in the best position to help our children identify their strengths, gifts, talents, and calling. We see what they're naturally good at — and what they're not so good at. We see what they're passionate about — and what they find boring. We see what work environments and tasks bring out the best in our children — and what environments kill their motivation.

It's hard work to see these things clearly, but no one is in a better place to recognize and identify these things in our children than us. Teachers, coaches, and youth pastors can certainly help, but they only see our children in limited contexts. We have an opportunity to see our children in a wide variety of contexts and help them discover the gifts, talents, and passions that their heavenly Father put in them before they were born.

So what does leadership development at home look like in real life?

My First Attempt at Leadership Development

For my oldest son, William, we quickly identified an interest in academics. Ever since preschool, William has been an enthusiastic, passionate learner. He was always the first to raise his hand in class — whether or not he knew the answer. He always asked a lot of questions — about everything. And he was the one son whom we didn't have to force to do his homework. In fact, sometimes we had to force him to stop studying!

We identified William's love of learning early on, but we didn't know how that would develop — we just knew that something was there.

Fast forward to college. William was at Lipscomb University studying and playing tennis. But in his second year, as I mentioned in chapter six, he seriously injured his ankle playing basketball and effectively ended his college tennis career. While rehabilitating his leg, William learned from a professor about an opportunity to do a semester abroad at the University of Oxford in England.

William applied, got accepted, and informed us. As always with his academics, he initiated this, not us.

We were excited for him to study abroad and grow intellectually at one of the oldest and most prestigious universities in the world. But there was a price tag. On top of the regular tuition that we paid for at William's school (some of which was covered by scholarships), we had to pay for travel and additional fees that come with studying abroad. It was expensive, but at the time, we saw it as an important opportunity for William to challenge himself academically and discover if this lifelong passion for learning might be worth pursuing further.

Long story short, William left for Oxford a discouraged athlete and returned an enthusiastic academic. And he never looked back. After graduating from Lipscomb with degrees in history and French, he returned to Oxford to earn a master's degree in medieval history. Today, he's at Vanderbilt University completing a PhD in Middle Eastern history. His long-term goal is a career in academics as a college professor. (Or as I like to say, a campus missionary fully supported by the university.)

My Second Attempt at Leadership Development

For my middle son, James, we discovered pretty early on that music was his passion. At the insistence of my wife, we enrolled all of our children in piano lessons when they turned six — something about developing discipline. William enjoyed piano and drums, but his interest faded a little in high school when he got busy with sports. Jonathan hated piano, and we let him quit after a few years — mainly so we wouldn't have to hear him practice. (It was not pleasant.) James not only enjoyed piano, but he soon wanted a guitar.

I bought James a cheap guitar from Cebu to see if this was a passing fad or a real passion. The consistent discipline he showed on that cheap guitar led to a Taylor guitar for his thirteenth birthday. In high school, James started to write songs. Most of the music I listened to at the time (Mozart and Miles) had no lyrics, so I didn't know if his songs were any good, but I recognized that he loved music and song-writing — and that this might be something that God had gifted him to do.

In college, James also played tennis at Lipscomb, like his older brother. But he remained passionate about music. During that time, we continued to invest in guitars and equipment, and I tried to connect him with guitarists and songwriters I met around the Every Nation world.

Today, James is a business owner by day and songwriter by night. He loves his day job, but he's still passionate about writing music — especially worship music. Ironically, his first song that was recorded was not a worship song, but a country song called "Whiskey Don't Leave" that appeared on the inaugural EP of rising Nashville-based country singer, Kirstie Lovelady. His grandfather would be proud.

My Third Attempt at Leadership Development

For our youngest son, Jonathan, identifying his gifts and talents was a comical process of elimination. Jonathan loved to learn, but he was bored to tears at school. He loved to read but hated homework. We practically bribed him to finish college. Jonathan took piano lessons like his older brothers, but he hated that too. Jonathan was really good at sports, but he didn't have the competitive drive or killer instinct of his older brothers. He was good enough to play Division I tennis, but never seemed to care if he or his team won or lost. And he was way too nice to his opponents — something his brothers would never be accused of.

Until he was about twelve, Jonathan's most obvious passion was reading and his greatest gift was his wild imagination. This was before the arrival of digital books, so we never had enough shelf space to hold all of Jonathan's books. He always read books that were several years beyond his grade level. In middle school, he was reading college economics textbooks.

I'll never forget the day he asked me to buy him Muhammad Yunus's classic on microfinance, *Banker to the Poor.* I was surprised by his request, but we were on a trip and I figured it would give him something to read on the plane. This book by the Nobel Prize-winning economist from Bangladesh sparked in Jonathan a serious passion for business and global development — I think they call it social entrepreneurship now.

Since that day, Jonathan has read voraciously about microfinance, global development, economics, entrepreneurship, and international markets. He read so many of these books in his teens that by the time he got to college, he had already read many of the books he was assigned to read in his business classes (maybe that's why he Facebook-chatted with us in Manila from his Nashville classes). By about fourteen, Jonathan had figured out what he was going to do with the rest of his life — make lots of money and give it all away to help the poor.

He started investing in the stock market when he was about twelve. And when he ran out of his own money, he asked his brothers if he could invest theirs. He and his brother James (who also has a passion for business) started their first business when Jonathan was a sophomore in college. They started their second business together when Jonathan was a senior. And Jonathan and James started their third business last year with their partner, Mark, when Jonathan was just twenty-four.

I am so proud of my sons, and I love the wide variety of gifts and talents that God has placed in each of them. From their first day in kindergarten until today, Deborah and I have prayed almost every day that William, James, and Jonathan would be godly leaders, not crowd-followers. We not only prayed they would be leaders, we told them to lead, we equipped them to lead, and we empowered them to lead.

When it comes to identification of strengths and gifts, parents can learn an important lesson from Sam Mussabini, the track coach in the 1981 Oscar-winning movie, *Chariots of Fire*. When British Olympic runner Harold Abrams asks the famous coach if he will help him run faster, Mussabini replies, "I can't put in what God's left out."

> We not only prayed our sons would be leaders, we told them to lead, we equipped them to lead, and we empowered them to lead.

God deposits gifts and talents in all of our children. The job of parents is to simply discover and develop what God put in their kids.

For William, this meant funding his studies overseas. For James, it meant buying him a guitar and paying for his lessons. For Jonathan, it meant buying him books (lots of them) and investing in his early business startups.

Our children need benefactors — parents who are invested in their future. Parents who will actively and skillfully help them discover the unique gifts and calling that God has for them. Parents who will help their children locate their story in the larger story of God's mission on earth.

INSTRUCTION IN THINGS THAT MATTER

In the church context, we recognize that identification is not the end of leadership development — it's just the beginning. Even if someone figures out what they're gifted and called to do, they still need to be trained. In fact, young leaders with big vision and no training are, at best, ineffective, and at worst, dangerous.

The same goes for our children.

As parents, our role in the leadership development of our children does not stop with helping them identify their gifts, calling, and talents. It's sad, but I know far too many parents who are expert encouragers and build up their children's dreams, but fail to provide them any instruction to help them realize their dreams.

If we want to see our children become the leaders and world-changers that God has called them to be, we have to provide instruction. Instruction is the place where gifts and talents are sharpened, where our children are given practical tools to be effective leaders one day. For potential church leaders and pastors, instruction usually involves seminary or a church-based ministry school.

But what does instruction look like in the context of parenting?

While this may seem obvious, formal education is crucial. Where you choose to send your children to school at each developmental stage will have a massive impact on how they develop as leaders. Why? Because school is where children are taught how to think.

Think about it. The primary reason our children study math, science, literature, and history is not so that they will know lots of math, science, literature, and history. The primary aim is to develop critical thinking skills.

The reason they're forced to learn long division is not so they can do complicated math problems if they don't have a calculator on hand. The process of working out a complicated math problem develops abstract problem-solving skills.

The reason children are forced to study history is not so they know about dates and dead people. We study history because history forces us to wrestle with questions of cause-and-effect and pushes us to think about the moral consequences of actions.

Unfortunately, too many schools and teachers focus entirely on content mastery and memorization, while failing to emphasize critical thinking.

It's up to us as parents to challenge our children to cultivate critical thinking skills and put them in an educational environment where critical thinking is valued and prioritized. If given the choice between a private Christian school and a secular public school, don't just assume that the school with the Christian brand is better. Take a serious look at which school prioritizes critical thinking.

Make no mistake — your children's education is your responsibility. And it's up to you and your spouse to choose the best educational option for your children. I won't attempt to tell you what the best option is. Public schools, private prep schools, Christian schools, homeschool, classical schools, online schools. Lots of options are out there. Don't let anyone tell you that one choice is more "biblical" than another. The decision is up to you and your spouse — and the right decision is always based on a combination of factors — quality of education, budget, commute, teachers, and perhaps most importantly, your individual child's needs.

My oldest son, William, went to the same Christian school in Manila (Faith Academy) from kindergarten until graduation. The school is affordable, has a dedicated faculty, and offered an international curriculum that ensured that William would be prepared for university education in America or Europe.

James and Jonathan started at Faith Academy, but in high school, Deborah and I put them in an online school, partially because of our ever-increasing travel schedule and partially to give them more time to devote to tennis. We never home-schooled our kids, but we didn't feel that we had to. We had great options. Also, we never put our children in Philippine public schools because we wanted them to be prepared for an American or European university education.

> It's up to us as parents to challenge our children to cultivate critical thinking skills and put them in an educational environment where critical thinking is valued and prioritized.

Our educational decisions were based on a complex variety of factors that were unique to our family. And your decisions about your children's education will be based on an equally complex variety of factors unique to your family. The most important thing is that you and your spouse make a thoughtful and prayerful decision based on what's best for your kids, not what someone else prescribes as God's way.

Are you and your spouse thoroughly engaged in this crucial aspect of your child's leadership development, or are you in default mode?

Your children will only be in primary school and high school once, so choose wisely.

Instruction Beyond the Classroom

School is not the only place where our children receive valuable instruction that helps them develop as leaders. It's only the starting place. If school is the place where our children are taught to cultivate critical thinking, then extracurriculars are often the place where our children have an opportunity to develop specific skills that help them maximize their gifts and talents.

In our family, this meant competitive sports (as opposed to recreational sports) and music lessons.

Our sons' after-school hours were dominated by baseball, basketball, tennis, music (especially for James and William), and art (for Jonathan). But we weren't filling our afternoons with music and sports just to keep our sons busy and out of trouble. Especially as they got older, we saw all the money and time spent on sports and music as an investment in our sons' future.

After a few years of baseball and basketball, we recognized that our sons were all gifted athletes who loved to compete. So when they all settled on tennis as their sport of choice, Deborah and I decided to invest in tennis. For each of my sons, the goal was to get an athletic scholarship to play tennis in college. This meant lots of hours on the court — and lots of money spent on coaches, equipment, and tournaments. It was worth it for us because we were thinking long-term.

The same logic applied to our sons' music and art lessons.

The discipline of learning an instrument or a sport is valuable in itself — whether or not your child ends up playing or performing at an elite level. I would encourage you, as parents, to be aware of your children's gifts and talents and interest—and insofar as it's in your budget—to provide opportunities for them to gain instruction that will help them develop those skills.

You never know what a piano lesson, an art lesson, or basketball practice might lead to.

IMPARTATION: INSTRUCTION ON STEROIDS

Impartation is a stage of leadership development that focuses on shaping the character, habits, and values of the leader. It's the elusive and invisible part of leadership development. If instruction is focused on training the mind of the leader, then impartation is focused on the heart. And if the typical setting for instruction is the classroom, music room, or playing field, the typical setting for impartation is everywhere else that real life happens.

In many ways, instruction and impartation are two sides of the same coin.

For example, when we signed our sons up for piano lessons, we hoped that they would learn how to the play the piano. Sight reading, a sensitive ear, finger dexterity—these are all skills that should come with piano instruction. But Deborah and I didn't sign our sons up for piano for these skills alone.

In many ways, it didn't really matter to us if our children became child prodigies—none of them did. There was something more that we wanted to impart to them during their years of piano instruction.

That something was discipline.

Much to my sons' dismay, weekly piano lessons came with daily piano practice (thirty minutes every day when they were younger and sixty minutes when they were older). And Deborah was a strict enforcer of piano practice. No playing with friends, no sports, no TV, no dinner until piano practice was finished. My sons — who didn't really mind weekly piano lessons — hated daily piano practice. The scales, the Twinkles (you'll know what I'm talking about if your kids did the Suzuki method), the trills, the arpeggios. Playing a new song intentionally slow — first with the right hand, then with the left. All of this while staring at a kitchen timer that never seemed to tick fast enough.

What were we trying to accomplish?

We were trying to teach our children the importance of consistent excellence in the small things — a.k.a. discipline. No one enjoys playing a song half time to a metronome with only the left hand. No one enjoys doing the same finger drills every day. No one enjoys struggling with the sheet music of a new song. Everyone wants instant and excellent results without the painful hours of practice.

Piano was one way that Deborah and I decided to impart discipline to our sons. We wanted them to understand that behind every beautiful song that someone played in a performance was hours of boring practice — consistent excellence in the small things when no one was watching. This was why piano was such an important part of our family life when my kids were growing up. We were definitely a sports family, but music provided an opportunity to develop new skills and most importantly, to develop discipline.

Attitude Adjustment

Compared to piano practice, it was much easier to get my sons to go to baseball and tennis practice, but sports still provided plenty of opportunities for impartation.

Maybe the most obvious example was sportsmanship.

In our baseball years, my sons were fortunate enough to be on some very good teams. In William's first five years of baseball, his team won the league championship three times and was runner-up twice.

We rarely lost.

> We wanted our children to understand that behind every beautiful song that someone played in a performance was hours of boring practice — consistent excellence in the small things when no one was watching.

In fact, William was so competitive and so unaccustomed to defeat that he cried almost every time his team lost (like once a season). Most of the time, Deborah and I simply tried to console our sons in their moments of defeat, but other times, these losses provided great opportunities to teach them the lost art of sportsmanship — a.k.a. how to be a gracious loser or a humble winner.

"William, I know that losing is terrible, but it's not the end of the world. There is no reason to let this loss ruin our lunch."

"James, I know you think that we should have won that game, but you still need to congratulate your friend on the other team for a good game."

"Jonathan, never throw your glove in the dugout."

"Steve [Deborah talking], never throw your clipboard in the dugout."

These lessons took years to sink in.

One thing I love about team sports is that children are forced to work with others. On a team, it's not about individuals being awesome on their own; it's about individuals working together and committing to the same mission and the same game plan.

One time, James and Jonathan signed up with a friend for a nationwide three-on-three basketball tournament held in the mall. James was pretty good at basketball, but what he really had going for him was his size. As a twelve-year-old, he was bigger and taller than most Filipinos his age. Jonathan was not a good basketball player, but he was an aggressive defender and rebounder — as long as he stayed out of foul trouble. Jonathan's friend Vico was a skilled basketball player, but he was a reluctant shooter and was happy to let James do most of the scoring.

When my sons came home from the first day of the tournament, they were proud to report that they had dominated the competition and had made it to the finals (which would be played the next day). I asked James how he played, and he told me that he scored sixty points in one game. I was proud and stunned at the same time. Then I asked Jonathan how many points he scored.

"Zero," Jonathan said. "James never passed me the ball."

"How many points did Vico score?" I asked.

"Four."

"So you guys won 64–55, and James scored sixty of your points?"

I recognized a parenting moment when I saw one. So I spoke with James privately about the importance of being a team player — or passing the ball on occasion.

"But I'm better than Jonny and Vico," replied James.

"It doesn't matter," I explained, "Good players learn how to include their teammates and make everyone better."

James wasn't too thrilled about the idea of sharing the ball, but he agreed to pass a little more in the championship game.

The next day, they lost a hard-fought championship game. But the real win was that Jonathan finally scored, and James registered his first assist of the tournament.

As parents, we must use successes and especially failures in sports, music, and academics as opportunities to shape our children's character. Whether it's discipline, sportsmanship, or the value of teamwork, we can't assume that our children will cultivate these things by default. Though coaches and teachers can also reinforce these values, it's up to us as parents to take responsibility to shape our children's character.

If your child is lazy in piano practice, why would you assume that he'll be excellent in the workplace when he grows up?

If your child acts like a jerk on the baseball field or the tennis court, why would you assume that he won't act the same way in a board meeting — or the church softball league?

If your child acts selfishly on the basketball court, why would you assume that he'll be a team player when he grows up?

If we want our children to be disciplined, gracious, team-oriented leaders one day, it's up to us to impart the right values to them when they're children. Whenever I corrected my sons' attitudes on the court or the field, it was never just about making them better athletes. It was always about making them better leaders.

INTERNSHIP AT HOME

When emerging leaders have identified their gifts and callings, and have had opportunities to grow through instruction and impartation, they need to go through a period of internship before they're launched into leadership.

Why?

> If we want our children to be disciplined, gracious, team-oriented leaders one day, it's up to us to impart the right values to them when they're children.

Because internship provides a safe place for leaders to get hands-on training and apply what they've learned. Internships allow emerging leaders to observe established leaders, work alongside them, and get helpful feedback from them as they venture out on their own.

Most people recognize that internships are an essential stage of leadership development, but how does this stage relate to parenting? What does internship look like in the home?

Obviously, we're not really talking about formal internships — like unpaid summer college interns. We're talking about how we can apply the same principles to the home. Applying this principle may take some creativity, but here are a few examples of how we made space for our children to grow as leaders while at home.

Household Chores. This may be too obvious to even list, but think about it. Parents have many reasons for having their children do chores. Some parents simply need an extra set of hands to clean. Others want to teach their children hard work. Still others want to introduce their children to the concept of work for pay through chores for allowance.

We saw household chores as leadership training.

How? Well, weekly chores gave us the opportunity to work alongside our children. Deborah and I weren't making them clean the patio furniture because we didn't want to clean it. We were making them clean the patio furniture with us, so they could observe the way we worked and gradually take responsibility for certain tasks around the house. If they cleaned the windows too quickly and carelessly, Deborah was always happy to give some constructive feedback and send them back to the windows for another round of cleaning.

William used to jokingly say that he was an expert at cleaning bird poop off of our patio fan. Why? Because he had cleaned that fan so many times that he began to see it as his responsibility. James claimed to be an expert at cleaning windows. And Jonathan developed a reputation as a speed-cleaner — though he also was notorious for having to re-clean after the inspector (his mom) checked his work.

Family Devotions. While we've already talked about the importance of family devotions in several different chapters, we can also talk about it in the context of leadership development.

When our sons were teenagers, Deborah had the idea to have each of our sons lead family devotions on different weeks. The first week of the month, Deborah or I would lead, then the next week William would lead, then the next week James, then the next week Jonathan.

This resulted in a wonderful season of family devotions when our sons got hands-on training in how to communicate spiritual truths and lead prayer. Our hope was that this season of "internship" would prepare them to one day lead family devotions in their own homes. They had seen us lead family devotions for years. This was their opportunity to participate as leaders and get constructive feedback and encouragement from us.

Taking Your Children to Work. Obviously, this is easier with some jobs than others. But if you have an opportunity to bring your children to work so they can see what you do for a living and how you work, it is well worth the effort.

When my sons were in elementary school, every now and then I would try to take one of them with me when I was visiting a church somewhere in Asia. For example, William went with me to Myanmar because he was good friends with the son of our pastor in Yangoon. James went with me to Indonesia because he was friends with the son of our pastor in Jakarta. And Jonathan went with me to Singapore because he wanted to go to the zoo.

I didn't take my sons on every trip. Just a few when the schedule and budget worked out. But these were always unique moments to spend one-on-one time with them and let them see what my job was really like.

It doesn't matter if your children end up doing the same job you do. What matters is that they have an opportunity to see you at work and to see how you work. These moments have the potential to shape how they view work and leadership when they grow up.

These are just a few examples of how we applied the principles of internship to leadership development in our own home.

But leadership development isn't just about your relation-ship with your kids. Sometimes it's about connecting them with people who can help them grow as leaders in a certain field. For example, over the years I've had the privilege of working with Stephen Mansfield, a bestselling author, historian, public intellectual, and friend.

As often as I can, I try to bring William along when I meet with Stephen. I first introduced him to Stephen when he was making a decision about where to apply for graduate school. I knew that Stephen, who has a PhD in history, would be a great person for William to talk with about this decision. I was happy to give him advice myself, but I knew that he needed other mentors in this field. William, who's a big fan of Stephen's work, has stayed in touch with Stephen and continues to ask him questions about academics and publishing.

GREAT EXPECTATIONS FOR THE NEXT GENERATION

Leadership development starts at home, but hopefully it doesn't end there.

If we do our jobs right as parents and raise our children to be leaders, their transition into the real world of work can be natural. In fact, it may seem like they grow up too quickly.

This can be how things work out, but it isn't the norm these days. Young people, even those that get college degrees, are less and less confident about what to do next after they finish college. Many get part-time jobs and move back home. Some take their entire twenties to "figure out" what they want to do with their lives. Nothing is necessarily wrong with getting a job at Starbucks or living at home to save on rent for a season. However, I would guess that this trend doesn't represent a coherent career strategy for most young adults. Rather, it represents an immaturity and lack of leadership development in young people.

That may sound harsh. But frankly, there's too much that needs to be done in the world for young people to delay getting in the game. I don't blame millennials for their seeming unwillingness to commit to a career. I don't blame them for their reluctance to take responsibility for their world. I don't blame them for living at home and delaying marriage and family and work.

I blame their parents — my generation.

It's up to us to raise children who are leaders. Like Pip, our children need benefactors — people who are invested in their future. People who have great expectations for them. People who are willing to make financial and relational sacrifices so that they can grow as leaders and world-changers.

DISCUSSION QUESTIONS

1. Looking back on your own childhood, do you feel like your parents were invested in your leadership development and preparing you for the future? Or did you have to look elsewhere for benefactors and mentors?

2. Have you and your spouse thought much about leadership development in your home? Practically, how can you help your children identify their gifts and talents and develop them?

3. Do you see your children as potential world-changers? Why or why not? What's your prayer for your kids?

AFTERWORD

ALL'S WELL THAT ENDS WELL
The Ultimate Goal

> *The web of our life is of a mingled yarn, good and ill together.*
>
>   William Shakespeare, *All's Well that Ends Well*

> *The end of the matter; all has been heard. Fear God and keep his commandments, for this is the whole duty of man.*
>
>   Ecclesiastes 12:13

> *And we know that for those who love God all things work together for good, for those who are called according to his purpose.*
>
>   Romans 8:28

A*ll's Well That Ends Well* was written in 1605 and published about twenty years later. It's sometimes classified as one of Shakespeare's comedies and sometimes as a tragedy. That's how parenting is, a combination of comedy and tragedy that often defies category.

Here's a quick summary of Shakespeare's *All's Well that Ends Well* comedy/tragedy.

Spanish peasant Helena is in love with rich Bertram, who hardly acknowledges her existence. By some quirk of fate or miracle of modern medicine, Helena helps heal the King and, as a royal reward, she is promised the husband of her choice. Naturally, she chooses Bertram, who naturally rejects her.

To get away from his love-crazed stalker, Bertram goes to war in Italy. Helena follows.

Borrowing an idea from Laban, who tricked Jacob into marrying Leah rather than Rachel, Bertram's girlfriend, Diana, helps Helena seduce Bertram. Helena then fakes her death, returns to Spain, and gets adopted by Bertram's mother. Of course, there are enough ridiculously tragic subplots to categorize *All's Well that Ends Well* as a Brazilian *telenovela* rather than a Shakespearian classic.

Eventually Bertram is won over by his obsessive stalker and pledges his undying love. So, all is well that ends well, right?

In many ways, Shakespeare makes a good point, and in many ways, he completely misses the point.

From an eternal perspective, I guess all's well that ends well. As long as our kids make it to heaven, by the grace of God, then all is well. In other words, even if we completely fail as parents, mess up our kid's lives, but they eventually find God (and their insurance includes lifelong therapy), the Bible promises that when they get to heaven, God will "wipe away every tear" and all will be well.

An eternal perspective is a good thing.

But our kids don't live in eternity — at least not yet. They live in time and space, and all will not be well from now until the end, unless parents get their hearts and their priorities right.

Even though Shakespeare's play ends with Helena getting her man, I'm not so sure they lived happily ever after, considering all the baggage they had to be carrying.

The better we do as parents, the less baggage our kids will carry throughout life, and the better chance they have of not only ending well, but having it go well with them from start to finish.

So, does that mean that our ultimate goal is for our kids to have a baggage-free life? That might be an admirable goal, but there's certainly a higher goal.

WATER SLIDES, SUNSETS, AND THE MEANING OF LIFE

I can't write or speak about the ultimate meaning of life without thinking about a conversation I accidentally over-heard at one of my favorite Philippine beaches almost twenty years ago.

"Come on, Daddy. Come down the slide with me."

Splash!

"It's fun, and see, the water's not too cold."

The overworked, stressed-out American executive mumbled to his young son while sipping some kind of crushed ice tropical concoction from a coconut shell. "Not now, son. I'm watching the sunset."

Like any normal ten-year-old, this kid couldn't even begin to understand how a human could choose to passively stare at a boring sunset rather than climb to the top of the slippery steps, stand in line behind a bunch of wet shivering kids, then speed down a water slide — eventually splashing into a pool full of rowdy pre-teens. So he asked: "Why are you watching the sun, Dad?" The boy wanted a simple, practical explanation to this unsolved middle-age mystery.

The dad waxed eloquent: "Because it's the meaning of life, son."

"The what?"

"The meaning of life." The philosopher-dad explained to his perplexed son, "When you're ten years old, waterslides and swimming pools are the meaning of life. But when you're forty, watching the sunset over Sombrero Island is the meaning of life. Understand?"

I don't think junior understood at all.

I'm not sure Dad understood the meaning of life either.

I certainly identify with the overworked, stressed-out American living abroad, trying to find a moment of rest on a Philippine beach. And I do appreciate beautiful sunsets, especially sunsets that slowly disappear over Sombrero Island. But for me, the meaning of life is much more than waterslides, sunsets, and tropical drinks.

That seaside sunset conversation started my mind racing about the real meaning of life. Immediately I thought about the 1991 comedy, *City Slickers*. In my favorite scene, Curly, a leather-faced cowboy, pointed his index finger straight in the air and spoke of the "meaning of life."

When the misplaced city slicker from New York City Mitch Robbins wondered how *one finger* could be the meaning of life, Curly explained that *one thing*, not one finger, is the meaning of life.

"One thing. What one thing?" the city slicker inquired.

"That's what *you* have to find," Curly responded.

"WHAT IS MAN'S CHIEF END?"

What's your one thing? What's the meaning of your life? Sunsets and vacations? Water slides and swimming pools? Money? Fame? Popularity? Success?

King David found his one thing. And, he didn't find it in fame, fortune, success, survival, or sunsets. He certainly had all of these — especially fame and fortune. But what was David's one thing? What was the meaning of his life? He left us a clue in Psalm 27:4: "*One thing* have I asked of the Lord, that will I seek after: that I may dwell in the house of the Lord all the days of my life, to gaze upon the beauty of the Lord and to inquire in his temple."

David's one thing was the presence of the Lord. From his days as a poor shepherd boy to his years in the palace as a rich and powerful king, David had a lifelong obsession with the glory and majesty of God.

The apostle Paul was another guy who discovered his one thing. Here's what he said about it:

"But whatever gain I had, I counted as loss for the sake of Christ. Indeed, I count everything as loss because of the surpassing worth of knowing Christ Jesus my Lord. For his sake I have suffered the loss of all things and count them as rubbish, in order that I may gain Christ . . . Brothers, I do not consider that I have made it my own. But *one thing* I do: forgetting what lies behind and straining forward to what lies ahead . . ." (Philippians 3:7,8,13).

Paul was a brilliant and highly educated man. He had power and status in the Jewish religious system. But he says he counted it all as nothing compared to knowing Jesus. He didn't toss it all in the trash for money or for ministry, but for Jesus. Paul's great passion in life was to know God.

According to David and Paul, the real meaning of life begins and ends with the pursuit of God. And just how does one pursue and find God? As with all other questions that matter, Jesus is the answer: "I am the way, and the truth, and the life. No one comes to the Father except through me" (John 14:6).

According to this Scripture, Jesus is more than the meaning of life—He is the life. Thus, any search for meaning apart from Jesus Christ is fruitless.

The Westminster Catechism summed it up as well as it could ever be summed up when it answered the question: "What is man's chief end?" The answer: "Man's chief end is to glorify God and to enjoy Him forever."

As important as family is, it's not the meaning of life and it's not humanity's chief end. If we define our lives by our families, we will ultimately miss the point. To glorify God and to enjoy Him forever is what gives life meaning. Once we pursue and discover the real meaning of life, then the sunsets are much more spectacular and the water slides with our kids are much more fun!

The Ultimate Goal

I end this discussion about the meaning of life and I end this book with one last story and one last Scripture that will hopefully help us all embrace life's only ultimate goal.

It was early Sunday morning. I was at my desk with my Bible wide open and my eyes half-closed. I could feel myself slipping into a trance—or was it a nap? As I put the finishing touches on my first sermon of 1997, suddenly the door flung open and my eleven-year-old son charged into my sleepy study, victoriously waving an index card in the air.

"Hey Dad, you wanna hear my goals for the new year?" He had obviously been inspired by his goal-setting mother.

"Sure William, I'd love to hear them." I closed my Bible, opened my ears and eyes as he confidently read his list.

"I have two kinds of goals this year. Spiritual goals and physical goals." I felt like I was hearing my first sermon of the year.

William continued his accidental sermon: "My spiritual goals are to read the whole New Testament, control my tongue, and put God first every day. And my physical goals are to make straight As, make the (basketball) all-star team, and be the fastest runner in the sixth grade."

As I thought about my son's goals for the year, I wondered if I should follow his lead and set some goals for a change. I've never been much of a goal-setter. One January, a few years ago, I did set a few goals, but I forgot about them until the following year, and never set goals again.

This year would be different. Inspired by my goal-setting son, I decided to present some really spiritual goals to the congregation for 1997.

Being a Bible teacher, my first step had to be a word study on goals. What did the Bible say about goal-setting anyway?

As I typed the word "goal" into my Bible software program, I sensed I was onto something big. Angels hovered around my PowerBook 1400c, with its gigantic one gigabyte hard drive and sixteen megabyte memory. After my PowerBook did its thing, one Scripture jumped off my screen and into my soul. I had found it, the ultimate goal for all parents for all time.

This ultimate biblical goal was explained in eight simple words in Paul's second letter to the church at Corinth.

When writing to the Corinthian church, Paul didn't say the goal was to double church attendance that year. The ultimate goal had nothing to do with baptismal numbers, mission offerings, or building programs.

Many of us aggressively pursue financial goals, retirement goals, and career goals while ignoring the ultimate goal. At times, some of us have lived as if the ultimate goal is to impress our parents, neighbors, and Facebook friends. Too many parents make it their goal to please their children.

So many good and godly goals scream for our attention every day, but there is only one ultimate goal. Here it is. The ultimate goal of life (and parenting), in the words of the apostle Paul: "We make it our goal to please him" (2 Corinthians 5:9, NIV).

If our ultimate goal is to please God, then all will end well with us, with our children, and with our children's children.

Living all of life to please God is how we discover the heart of parenting.

ACKNOWLEDGMENTS

I owe a debt of gratitude to many people for the lessons and stories in this book. I also owe a debt of gratitude to a few for the fact that this book actually got written and published.

Thank you to all the Victory Manila kids' ministry teachers and youth pastors (especially Gemma Hashmi, Joel Magpantay, Omeng Cervantes, Paolo Punzalan, and Rico Ricafort) who helped our sons become the men they are today.

Thank you to our many Every Nation friends around the world who have always treated our sons like your own (especially the Austin, Bonasso, Bonifacio, Broocks, Fabregas, Fuller, Gutierrez, Houston, Laffoon, Nubla, and Stewart families). You have helped our family more than you know.

Thank you to our other good friends around the world who also treated us and our sons like family (especially the Berry, Cannistraci, Chase, Long, Lyons, Mullen, and Quinley families). We learned so much from each of you and appreciate you always opening your doors to our family.

Thank you to the dedicated Faith Academy teachers, administrators, and coaches for providing strong academic foundations and a healthy spiritual environment for missionary kids.

Thank you to the talented teachers who taught William to play drums, James to play guitar, Jonathan to paint, and all three to play piano.

Thank you to all the baseball coaches, basketball coaches, and tennis coaches who taught our sons discipline, competition, and sportsmanship.

Thank you to our extended family — the Brooks, Drummonds, Holtons, McAfees, Murrells, Suells, and Wilkies for being the best grandparents, great-grandparents, uncles, aunts, and cousins.

Thank you, William, for making this book happen. If not for your research, discipline, writing skills, encouragement, and commitment, this book would exist only as random notes in my Moleskine.

Thank you, Rachel, for applying your sharp editorial eye to this project. And thank you for taking the job as my executive assistant. My life is more ordered, productive, and peaceful since you started working for me.

And finally, thank you, Deborah, for making all of us better. Our sons would not be the men they are without you. Neither would I. Doing life, family, and ministry with you has been indescribably amazing.

ABOUT THE AUTHOR

Steve Murrell is the cofounder and president of Every Nation Churches & Ministries, a church planting movement with a vision to plant churches and campus ministries in every nation. So far, Every Nation has planted churches in sixty-nine countries.

In 1984, Steve and his wife, Deborah, went to the Philippines for a thirty-day mission trip that turned into thirty years and counting. They are the founding pastors of Victory Manila, one church that meets in fifteen congregations across Metro Manila and has planted churches in over sixty Philippine cities and twenty-two nations. Today, Victory has more than 8,000 discipleship groups that meet in coffee shops, offices, campuses, and homes throughout Metro Manila.

Steve is the author of *WikiChurch* and *100 Years From Now*, and coauthor of *The Purple Book*, a foundational Bible study with more than one million copies in print.

Steve serves on the board of the Real Life Foundation, a Christian nonprofit that seeks to provide underprivileged Filipino youth with a better future by transforming their communities and giving them access to a good education.

After living in the Philippines for twenty-four years, Steve and Deborah now split their time between Manila and Nashville. Their first, second, and third attempts at parenting were born and raised in the Philippines and now reside in the United States.

For more information, blogs, social media, and podcasts, visit stevemurrell.com.

What will our movement look like 100 years from now?

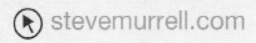

Jesus told us to go and make disciples.
Where do we start?

Start here.

WIKICHURCH
By Steve Murrell

HAVE YOU DONE THE **PURPLE BOOK**?

MAKE A DECISION THAT LASTS FOREVER

THE **PURPLE** BOOK

Biblical Foundations for Building Strong Disciples

RICE BROOCKS
STEVE MURRELL

☑ Develop solid biblical foundations.
☑ Grow strong in your Christian life.
☑ Stand firm in God's Word.

EVERY NATION

To order copies of The Purple Book, email orders@everynation.org.ph